What Others Are Saying About Jennifer Michelle and *The Light Bulb Effect*

"Jennifer is a true inspiration to anyone feeling broken by the blows of life. *The Light Bulb Effect* is the ultimate roadmap to putting the pieces back together and coming back stronger than ever!"

Dr. Taylor Clark
Best-Selling Author of *Beating All Odds*

"This book is written from the heart. And it is deep within the heart that we find hope, faith, courage, forgiveness, peace, truth, and unconditional Love. With imagination and creativity, Jennifer guides us through all of this."

John J. Murphy
Award-Winning Author and Business Consultant

"This book provides a map for comfort, peace, and healing for those going through hurt or those helping others who may be going through difficult times."

John Webster
Publishing and Marketing Coach and Author of *Mastering Your Fate*

"We all have our own stories and struggles, and we often feel alone in the journey of healing. *The Light Bulb Effect* makes you feel like someone who truly understands is there to walk with you on the path to becoming the best version of yourself."

Wendy Alexandre
The Results Boss

"*The Light Bulb Effect* isn't merely another book about change. It's a practical, step-by-step guide to take with you on the change journey. Jennifer's use of exercises makes *The Light Bulb Effect* a truly effective tool to drive real change."

Paxton Tupper
Meridian, Idaho

"An extraordinary call to embrace life's limitless potential! *The Light Bulb Effect* fearlessly challenges readers to raise the bar of their existence, leaving them inspired and empowered to embrace every moment with renewed passion and purpose."

Sheila Moore
My Mortgage Lady

"A true breath of fresh air! In a world saturated with information, *The Light Bulb Effect* gives you what you need to clear a path for your future; then it guides you in building your own framework to walk this path, giving you the tools to create beauty from brokenness."

Jake A. Marshall
The Ministry Lab Podcast

"If you're searching for answers to the difficulties in your life, let *The Light Bulb Effect* shed light onto your darkness. Jennifer Michelle shares her personal stories and the powerful practices she has developed and used to bring peace to a life that was once in pieces. Let her show you how you can also make your own light bulb whole."

Patrick Snow
Publishing Coach and International Bestselling Author of *Creating Your Own Destiny* and *The Affluent Entrepreneur*

"No one can deny the truth that life at times can be so hard we feel like we have shattered. In *The Light Bulb Effect*, Jennifer Michelle cleverly uses light bulb and light and darkness metaphors to demonstrate how sometimes we need to change our light bulb to be able to see our life as we want it to be and then take action to make that life our reality. Let this book provide you with the light you need.

Nicole Gabriel
Author of *Finding Your Inner Peace* and *Stepping Into Your Becoming*

"It's time you see the light. This book will show you how. Jennifer Michelle will walk you through how to change your broken life into a whole one so that your light never dims again. From discovering your strengths and embracing your brokenness to boundary setting and empowerment, *The Light Bulb Effect* contains something to benefit everyone! The only problem is you may be blinded by its brilliance!"

Tyler R. Tichelaar, PhD
Award-Winning Author of *Narrow Lives* and *The Best Place*

"Jennifer Michelle has written a must-read self-help book for anyone wanting to journey through personal growth and positive change. Read this book—and learn from one of the best."

Kari Brandt
San Jose, California

THE LIGHT BULB EFFECT
Finding Peace After Life Has Broken You Into Pieces

Published by:

Aviva Publishing
Lake Placid, NY
(518) 523-1320
www.AvivaPubs.com

Address all inquiries to:
Jennifer Michelle
1799 N. Lakes Place
Meridian, ID 83646
(208) 888-5905
jennifer@jennifermichellecoaching.com
www.LightBulbEffect.com
www.JenniferMichelleCoaching.com

978-1-63618-287-2 (softcover)
978-1-63618-288-9 (hardcover)
978-1-63618-289-6 (ebook)
Library of Congress Control Number: 2023913790

Editing: Superior Book Productions
Cover Design and Interior Book Layout: Nicole Gabriel, Angel Dog Productions
Author Photo: Cy Gilbert

Every attempt has been made to properly source all quotes.

Printed in China

First Edition

2 4 6 8 10 12

A HEALING JOURNEY TO FINDING YOUR INNER-LIGHT

THE Light Bulb EFFECT

FINDING PEACE AFTER LIFE HAS BROKEN YOU INTO PIECES

JENNIFER MICHELLE, MS

DEDICATION

To my amazing children, Averie and Noah.

Without you, life would not be the same. You make everything better, and I am a better person because I get the privilege of being your mom. Being your mom has been the greatest joy of my life.

ACKNOWLEDGMENTS

Many people helped me achieve the lifelong goal of writing this book. The following people were essential to making this dream a reality. I will forever be thankful to them.

Thank you to my mentor, Dr. Taylor Clark, for suggesting I take intentional steps to begin this process. Without your encouraging words and belief in my ability, I would never have started. Jessica Housel, you have always been the encouraging voice in my head from day one, keeping me going even when I felt I could not continue. To my aunt and uncle, Steve and Lauri Wilson, your support helped me push through the tougher times. You have both always been in the background quietly supporting me since I was a little girl.

To my past mentors—Jim and Lori Putman, Bill and Jill Krause, Jamie Lambert, and John Greenlee. Though you may not know how much crossing paths with you changed my life, I will be forever grateful for the examples you set by being your strong, authentic, genuine, empathetic, and compassionate selves. I am a better person today for spending time with each of you.

To those no longer with us—Grandma Ruth, Nical Preston, Kerry Dykstra, Dan Stults, and Thomas Shane Kirkham. Grandma Ruth was a Holocaust survivor with whom I spent every summer when I was growing up. I will always miss you. Your strong sense of self and all our late-night card games continue to inspire me. Nical Preston, I hope to one day see you again and have another conversation. Kerry, Dan, and Shane, you were loved and will be missed by so many. Having people like you in the world inspires us all.

Thank you to the professionals who held my hand along the way—my publishing coach Patrick Snow, my designer Nicole Gabriel, my editors Tyler Tichelaar and Larry Alexander, and Susan Friedmann of Aviva Publishing. Having a team of upstanding, experienced, caring, and proactive professionals around me as I went through this process often helped encourage me to keep going! Each of you played such a valuable role in helping me create this book and the content within it. I am forever changed because of your wise words, insightful advice, caring support, and introduction of new ideas. I will keep what I have learned from all of you with me as my own journey continues. Thank you.

CONTENTS

Introduction:	Understanding the Peace Among the Pieces	17
Section 1	**Discovering the Journey to Healing**	**25**
Chapter 1	Shining Light on Your Past, Present, and Future	27
Chapter 2	Becoming Familiar with Your Strengths	43
Chapter 3	Illuminating Your Development	51
Chapter 4	Discovering Your Authentic Self	61
Section 2	**Defining the Pieces of the Light Bulb**	**71**
Chapter 5	Investing in Your Light	73
Chapter 6	Embracing the Broken Pieces	83
Chapter 7	Creating Room for Growth	93
Chapter 8	Seeking the Light	103
Section 3	**Recognizing the Peace of the Light Bulb**	**111**
Chapter 9	The Hurt Light Bulb	113
Chapter 10	Finding Peace in the Pieces	127
Chapter 11	Holding Space for Healing	135

Section 4	**Developing the Light Bulb of Leadership**	**145**
Chapter 12	Sharing Your Light	147
Chapter 13	Transformational Change	157
Chapter 14	The Light Bulb of Empowerment	165
Chapter 15	The Light Bulb of Service	177
Section 5	**Identifying Life Transitions**	**187**
Chapter 16	The Light of Relationship	189
Chapter 17	The Light of Parenting	201
Chapter 18	The Light of Friendship	215
Chapter 19	The Light of Life Events	227
Chapter 20	The Dim Light of Grief	237
Section 6	**Sustaining the Future**	**249**
Chapter 21	The Light of Career	251
Chapter 22	The Light of Finances	261
Chapter 23	The Light of New Beginnings	269
A Final Note:	Taking the Light of Action	275
About the Author		281
The Finance Diet		285
Book Jennifer Michelle to Speak at Your Next Event!		287

Introduction

UNDERSTANDING THE PEACE AMONG THE PIECES

"Many of life's failures are people who did not realize how close they were to success when they gave up."

— Thomas Edison,
American Inventor

Are you hurting due to circumstances that dimmed your light? Do you feel like you can't escape the darkness, leaving you feeling tired, afraid, or broken? If this situation resonates with you, know you are not alone. Though the path may seem dark, there is light to be found. Though hope may seem hidden, a healing journey awaits you. The hurt you have experienced is not the end. Until you find the hope, let me carry it for you. As you read this book, I will give you insight into healing paths you can take, and we will do this together. Remember, the light you desire could be just around the corner; until you find it, don't give up! Keep trying. When you fail, try again. In failure, there is hope—hope of a better future—and together, we will find it!

DISCOVERING THE LIGHT

As I tightened the bright green light bulb into place for our Halloween decorations, it shattered in my hand. Looking down, I saw shards of glass everywhere and a problem that needed to be fixed. Just as that light bulb started out whole with a purpose, so did you. No one in this world is unbroken, but the exciting fact is that in your brokenness, you can find your light, your purpose, and your passion. Think back to some of the times you felt betrayed, broken, or mistreated. Everyone can relate to these feelings because they are all more common than any of us care to show.

Maybe you have experienced loss in your career. You might have lost a loved one—a child, partner, parent, friend, or family member. Maybe you have been the unfortunate victim of neglect or mental, physical, sexual, or emotional abuse. You might have experienced an affair, betrayal, or loss of trust. Whatever hurts that you carry, your brokenness is not the end of your story. In your brokenness lies unexpected beauty. There is no foundational purpose to you being broken. You were not intentionally broken by the "powers that be" so you could be light to others in the world, as I often hear people say to those who are hurting. Hearing such feedback can be really damaging; the person then begins to question why hurt must happen at all. Choices were made—just like with me screwing in the light bulb—that resulted in hurt.

Once you begin to realize your value is still there after the brokenness, you can begin to heal and move forward. That is not to say you won't become light for those who are also hurt. You may discover yourself finding comfort in others' experiences of hurt as you learn how they got through the hurt. People who have been hurt—who have gone through the work of healing, who feel comfortable and confident being vulnerable, and who choose to share their journey of hurt and healing—can become inspirers. These people are valued because they can be an example of how you can continue after experiencing hurt and loss.

You can learn from people who share their stories of hurt. But hurt was not intentionally allowed in that individual's life by the "powers that be" just so they could be the light to someone else. If that were the case, why would hurt have to happen at all? Someone made a choice, and hurt was the outcome. Brokenness happens, but be assured, healing happens also, and there is hope! If you are hurting now, or if you have already gone through a journey of hurt and healing, think about sharing your story. It could inspire others who feel like they are stuck in the dark. Of course, some stories are just too painful to share and best left in the dark. If healing has been accomplished, choosing whether to share is a personal choice that should be made by you.

PAVING THE PATH FORWARD

Coming from a family with multiple divorces and cracks in the "bulb," I had the powerful desire to achieve success and pave a different path. As I grew older, I held strongly to the belief that I did not want to end up like others I had witnessed. In high school, I heard a speaker who talked about what I assumed was their perfect life. I thought I could never achieve the fantastic things they had found on their journey to success. Success is interesting because people define it differently, but ultimately, they are all searching for the foundational concept of a happy life.

Doubt can rob you of the actual reality of the amazing things you can accomplish. Had it not been for a couple of extremely strong mentors, I would not be where I am today. Those mentors taught me an amazing survival skill: If I felt like I could not do something, all I had to do was find someone who knew how to do the thing I wanted to do and ask them for help. Sometimes that meant paying for services such as business coaching, mentoring, and counseling. If there is something you would like to accomplish, but you don't think you can, you are wrong. You just need to find the right person to walk the journey with you and show you how to do the thing.

In a seminar I attended in Washington, DC, a speaker shared a gem of knowledge I have never forgotten: If you see another person achieving something, you can do it too. If it is humanly possible and you want to learn how, with enough work, it can be within your reach. Never believe otherwise. You may feel like a broken light bulb, but that doesn't mean your pieces are less valuable.

In this book, you will learn how your brokenness can become your strength and how you can accomplish things you dream about. You will learn about the concepts of brokenness, strength, and success, and how these concepts apply to various parts of your life so you can achieve the things you set out to achieve. Life does break us into pieces at times; getting back to your peace is a journey that needs to be intentional, authentic, and filled with vulnerability and self-kindness. Failure is an important part of your journey, and the only way you will truly remain broken is if you choose to stop trying. There is peace for you to find and experience.

As you read, I encourage you to highlight sentences and sections in this book that provide you with hope. Then if (and when) you find yourself struggling in the future, you can reread these sections to give yourself a boost of inspiration. If you apply the wisdom and knowledge you gain from this book to your everyday life, you will be on your way to finding a stronger foundational sense of peace that will help lead you to achieve the things you desire. The purpose of this journey is not to become whole again because that is a difficult task. The purpose is to find your peace among your pieces. People all have pieces. You are not alone. No one goes through this world without scratches, scars, and broken glass, but with the hope, knowledge, and skills you discover in this book, you will be able to navigate your journey toward a happier, healthier foundation.

JUMPING TOWARD THE LIGHT

Knowing that I don't have all the answers, I have written this book for you as a "jumping off point" to inspire you and provide a level of ongoing hope that will motivate you to take the next step in your journey to success. I believe in you, and I believe you can do it! Just like you, I have experienced brokenness on my journey to success. Just like you, I am human and have made mistakes big and small. My journey started the instant I felt like a mentor believed in me. That journey took me on to college, then graduate school where I earned my Master's in Marriage and Family Counseling. When I was younger, I never thought I would even earn a bachelor's degree. After graduating with my master's, I opened Family Counseling Services in Meridian, Idaho, in 2008. Today, I have a staff that averages twenty-five full-time employees. I share all this to show you it can be done. You can achieve the goals you want to. Don't let anyone make you believe anything less. You've got this; you always have—you just might not have known it until now.

You might still be carrying doubts even as you read this. Know those doubts are natural and, in fact, can help motivate you toward your goal. Those doubts cause you to ask important questions, and you will find your brain starting to engage. Your brain will start to think about answers to those doubts and can even help you overcome the obstacles in your path. Do not be afraid of the doubts! Embrace them, and if they become intrusive, grab a journal and a pen and write them down. Get them out of your brain and onto paper.

Having doubts is one way your brain is working through the possible scenarios and answers to the roadblocks you face. It is okay if you don't have all the answers right now. If you come upon a roadblock you cannot overcome, ask for help. You can do this by spending time with a friend or family member, or through more official actions such as business mentoring or counseling. Remember, we are all broken—every one of us. Even in your brokenness, you can achieve your goals and find success. Keep going and you will rise above. I believe in you. I believe you can do it! I believe you can accomplish the things that may have only felt like far-off dreams in the past. Take one step at a time, and when you need help, ask—do not quit. You can do this. You've got this!

TAKING A MENTORING APPROACH

Going forward, I want to be your mentor, coach, source of inspiration, and accountability partner. You may experience various emotions as you read different sections of this book. Come to this book when you feel sad, inspired, or ready to act. Take a break from this book when you feel you have what you need for the day, when you want to stop and do work on some of the tasks, or when you need a break from the subject you are reading about. Be assured, this book is written for you; this is your journey to go through at the speed you feel comfortable. Life is a journey with ups, downs, broken pieces, and peace…among all the other things you experience throughout your life.

Are you ready? Take a deep breath, and let's begin this journey together. Reading this book for the first time? Enjoy the journey and go through it at your own pace. As the characters in the movie *Night at the Museum: Secret of the Tomb* say:

Larry (Ben Stiller): I have no idea what I'm going to do tomorrow.

Teddy (Robin Williams): How exciting!

Jennifer Michelle

Jennifer Michelle

Section 1

DISCOVERING THE JOURNEY TO HEALING

"The journey of a thousand miles begins with one step."

— Lao Tzu,
Chinese Philosopher

Chapter 1

SHINING LIGHT ON YOUR PAST, PRESENT, AND FUTURE

"The heritage of the past is the seed that brings forth the harvest of the future."

— Wendell Phillips, American Reformer
(In 1881, Phillips gave a speech that William E. Sawyer transcribed in time to print the next morning in the *Boston Globe*. The article was called "Voices for Freedom.")

Thomas Edison received a patent for his light bulb on January 27, 1880, but he was not the only one working on creating light using a filament (the little piece of wire in the bulb that produces the light). In 1835, the first constant light was produced. Dozens of scientists over the years from 1835 tried until Edison was able to produce the first practical, long-lasting, high-resistance carbon filament. In fact, Thomas Edison found himself in some legal trouble with both William E. Sawyer and Albon Man—who worked together on several patents for light bulbs. Edison's path to inventing his incandescent light bulb featuring a high-resistance, commercially viable carbon filament was paved with his own intelligence and that of his associates at Menlo Park and his competitors. Many have said Edison thrived and did his best when he faced competition.

Just like Edison's invention has a past, present, and future, so do you. Your journey has included successes and failures, ups and downs, allies and enemies. All these ingredients are part of the recipe that helped make your success. They are part of your journey, and whether good or bad, you would not be where you are today without having those pieces in your life. You may have experienced the most beautiful upbringing, or you may have been brought up in a home that was far from a fairytale. You may have easily found the love of your life, or you may have had to experience some bumps in the road. You may have made the most amazing decisions on the way to your career, or you may have had to go through some trials to get to where you are today.

Whatever your journey has been, the present is here, and the future is still yours to create. That is the ultimate beauty of invention. If something is not working the way you want it to, you can choose to invest time and effort right now, in the present, to turn it around and make something better in the future. If you don't lose hope for a better future, and you are willing to put the work into the present, you really can accomplish even more than you set out to achieve.

In 2019, as a single mom, I was tasked with decorating for Halloween. I was eager to make the holidays special for my children. I had been single since 2016 and had found I could do a surprisingly excellent job with holiday prep. At Halloween, I was screwing in a green light bulb to set the ambiance for the decorations, when it shattered in my hand. It caught me off guard, and for a moment, I felt completely discouraged. Then I had an epiphany. I looked at the pieces of green shattered glass on the ground, and as I started picking them up carefully, I thought to myself how much I related to this small light bulb, once whole but now broken. At that very moment, a metaphor came to my mind about how we all start out whole, but through life's journey, we get scratches, scars, and sometimes even break. I grabbed a paper towel and decided to keep the pieces of this light bulb in my office as a reminder that even in my brokenness, there is still hope. To this day, I have that white paper towel with those pieces of broken light bulb displayed in my office to remind me that not everything will go my way, but even when things go badly, there is beauty in my pieces.

In that moment, looking at the shattered pieces on the floor, I realized that in my brokenness, hope for the future remained, and I would rather carry hope than continue to choose to feel broken. The power was within me, and how I approached my future was fully up to me.

I quickly grabbed some paper and began writing down some of these thoughts. As time passed, each time I walked by the broken pieces of that light bulb, more metaphors came to me. As often as I could, I wrote down the thoughts I was having about those glass pieces, and that is how this book began—with the realization that I would rather embrace my brokenness and know there is beauty and hope in the pieces than try to hide my brokenness from myself and the world.

Sometimes, you need to experience a breakdown to experience a breakthrough. Sometimes you will get scratches, scars, or wounds, but the truth is, beauty and hope for a better future lie in those setbacks.

REFLECTING ON THE PAST

Think about your dreams from when you were younger. What did you hope to achieve? What were your heart's desires, dreams, and wishes? How did you want to make the world a better place? What was your light bulb? Set this book aside for a couple of minutes and complete the activity below to set your intentions for the rest of the time you will be investing in yourself as you go through the following chapters.

EXERCISE

Get a piece of paper and answer the following questions. Don't answer with what you know you "should" write down—answer from your heart, from the place you keep your dreams, your inner desires. This is a heart exercise, not a head exercise:

1. What did you dream of becoming when you were younger?
2. What about that dream made you think it would create happiness?
3. What elements of that dream do you continue to carry with you today?
4. What elements of that dream continue to provide hope?

Many of us did not become the person we imagined in our dreams, but the elements of our "younger dreams" stay in our hearts as we grow. In writing your answers, think about your dreams and how they helped you believe they would create happiness. Though the dream may not have been realized, your search for happiness continued. Though you might not have become the astronaut, pop singer, movie star, etc. you dreamt about when you were five, the ambition to think you could do amazing things is still in your heart.

The journey *restarts* now. The journey to believing in yourself again, just like you did when you were younger carrying around incredible dreams, restarts today. It is a journey of hope, healing, and success, and it starts now.

Accomplishment takes work. The light bulb was not invented on the first try. After others had tried for nearly eighty years, it still took Edison hundreds upon hundreds of attempts to develop the long-lasting, high-resistance carbon filament that made the light bulb commercially viable and lit up the world. So, put on your thinking pants, start believing you can do it, and get ready to do the work!

SHINING LIGHT ON YOUR PAST

Continuing along the road of shining light on your past, it's time to start healing old wounds. You carry coping skills that helped you get through challenging times. They probably served you well or you would not have used them. As you grew, those same coping skills may have become outdated and caused more damage than healing. Many continue to use outdated coping skills because they worked before, and believe they will continue to work, not realizing the exact opposite is true.

What worked when you were younger just does not work now because your situation has changed. Your environment, your developmental stage, and your intellectual ability have all changed, altering the effectiveness of past coping skills. Just as you mature as you live life, so should your coping skills mature. You no longer used a sippy cup once you learned how to drink from a regular glass. Part of this journey is realizing it is time to update the ways you look at and approach life. It is time to update and deepen the coping skills that will help you achieve success and the goals you set for yourself.

You have probably gone through some truly difficult trials with family, friends, and/or loved ones. Maybe you were divorced. Maybe you were mistreated by those meant to protect you. You may have had to take care of the people who were supposed to take care of you. You might have been a victim of a crime, abuse, or neglect. Maybe you faced an affair, a death, or heartache. No one is untouched by pain if they live long enough. Pain visits everyone occasionally, and it will decide now is your time more than once. As you continue to reflect, answer the following questions:

1. Which hurts are you holding on to that no longer serve you?
2. Where has anger gotten in the way of success, of reaching your goals, of believing there is hope for accomplishing the things you have always wanted to achieve?
3. What is the ultimate roadblock to taking the next step? What is keeping you from taking the first step toward doing the thing or things you know will bring you hope in your everyday life?

These can be tough questions, but you must answer them to heal your heart and the hurt you carry, which blocks you from achieving the things you desire. Give yourself time to reflect on the above questions. Make a safe space in your thoughts to explore your answers. Take precious time to sit in silence and reflect on the thoughts flowing through your mind. If you can give these thoughts space and time, you will help your body heal from the thoughts that have held you back.

Answers can come in silence. When you keep yourself too busy, you have no time for self-reflection, which can hinder the healing process. It is difficult to sit with your thoughts, especially those that bring up hurt, but trust in this process. Be kind to yourself and go where your thoughts lead. And when beneficial, pause for a moment; take a break.

WALKING THE JOURNEY

Some journeys are not meant to be walked alone. Some weights are not meant to be carried by just one person. When the journey seems dark and the weight seems too heavy, it is time to consciously decide to search for light. When you are feeling the heaviness of your situation, and it is becoming overwhelming, your body and mind will try to motivate you to find someone to help carry the burden. Sometimes carrying the burden is as easy as finding someone who will just listen to you talk about your struggle. Reaching out could mean calling a close friend or talking to family. Other times, you may need something more consistent, like the kind of support found in regularly scheduled professional counseling.

No one is untouched by hurt. When we are in the dark too long, reaching for help is reaching for light, and the light is where hope lives. It's like asking someone to bring sunshine into your darkness. Don't be afraid to ask when you need the sunshine. Be concerned if your thoughts are telling you not to ask. Light makes our concerns lighter. Don't let the darkness trick you into believing you are all alone. When you ask someone to share their light, you will be surprised at how many people are standing beside you—people you never noticed because the dark was telling you that you were alone. In reality, you were on a journey toward the light.

THE PRESENT

As Wendell Phillips said, "The heritage of the past is the seed that brings forth the harvest of the future." When you feel you have been buried by all life's dirt and it feels like the present is hopeless, realize you have a decision to make. This moment can be one of the most powerful in your life. You have the power to decide to stay in the dirt like a seed that never grows. You can choose to remain in your current situation, deciding it is good enough. You can choose to live this life and be okay. But in thinking about yourself as a seed, begin to realize that in the dirt, you can also begin to grow. This could be the moment you decide to start growing. This could be the moment you decide staying in the dirt is no longer enough. This could be the moment you decide to change the rest of your life by choosing to act, invest in yourself, and take the second step to becoming the person you know you can be. You have already taken the first step by investing your time and energy in reading this book. This action alone has started your journey to finding more light in your world. You are already on your way. The time is now. Embrace your path!

You will evolve your own being as you go through life. Just like the light bulb was not invented on the first round of attempts—it had to evolve to find success—so you will have to make the journey to find success. How you define success will be different than how others define it. Most people incorporate happiness in their definition of success, but each person defines happiness differently. To continue your journey, answer the following questions about your *present* to help identify what's going well for you right now and what you would like to work on.

EXERCISE

1. Free write—let your throughs go where they take you. Spend some time writing and journaling about your idea of success. How do you define it presently? How do you experience it? How have you been finding it and interacting with it? Do you find it more easily in some places than others? Is it achieving professional goals? Family goals? Do you find it in a hobby? Do you find it through service?
2. Develop a list of all the things you are currently happy about. It can be things that provide happiness and/or things you create and invest in that equate to greater happiness.

Your answers to the above questions are your strengths. As you continue, remember those answers. Go back to what you wrote when you feel weak. Put some of your answers on a sticky note and post it somewhere you will see it every morning. Personal growth does not always come without some confronting hurt. In those times, being able to go back to what makes you happy and helps you find and create joy can be the light your journey needs. When your journey is getting dim, go back to the things you wrote above and learn to pull strength from those items. Those things you listed are your sunshine, your light. They are your strength. Draw near to them.

FINDING GREATER LIGHT

As you continue down this road to finding greater light, remember to invest in the light you already have. The exercise above helped you identify the light in your life. As you go through this journey, don't neglect the things that currently give you strength. Do not lose them. Invest time, effort, and energy into them. Did you list a friend? Give them a call and schedule a lunch. Spend time with them; grow that light. Did you list an activity or hobby that helps you feel the light? Schedule more time to do that activity. Maybe you listed quiet time, alone time, or silence as things that bring you light. These are essential times, especially for introverts. If you identify as an introvert, invest time in yourself. Schedule a self-date, a night where you pick up dinner, read a book, or get tea alone to recharge your battery.

More than anything else, whatever you listed above, spend time maintaining, growing, and investing in those things.

CALL TO ACTION

Choose one thing from the above list and intentionally invest in it this week. It doesn't have to be a financial commitment. Offer a time commitment. Not all investments revolve around money. Get creative. Investing in one of these things is not only investing in that item; it is investing in strengthening your light, your source of power, your source of energy. It is true that if you are not ensuring your health, it is very difficult to ensure those around you are healthy. Like on a plane, put your oxygen mask on first. If you pass out, you can't help anyone. Take care of yourself so you can help others feel good too.

Making sure you are healthy, strong, and successful is also a blessing to those around you. When you are all those things, you set an example to those around you. It helps inspire them, shows them it can be done, and provides hope. Investing in yourself is an investment in those around you. Investing in your happiness inspires others. When you see a mentor succeed, someone who has really influenced you, it shows you that you can do it. Investing in yourself has the same effect on those who look up to you. They will see your success, your happiness, and your accomplishments and believe they can find those things too. You make the world around you better when you make yourself better—you bring much needed light into the world. Don't fear finding the light. Don't stay in the darkness. Now is your moment. Act now.

THE FUTURE

Here you go. The time is now. You have come a long way! You have looked at your past and present, and now it's time to do some fun work by dreaming about the future. The future is about your wishes, your desires, and your hopes. The future is about the light you want in your life. You can accomplish so much more than you ever thought. If something is humanly possible, you can accomplish it. Those who have done great things are no different than you. Accomplishment involves hard work, dedication, and ambition. You must be willing to put in the work, time, effort, dedication, and passion. You've got this! You can do it. Let's begin.

Think five years into the future. Take a moment to visualize where you are. What about ten years from now? What about even twenty years? Don't think practically; dream big. What do you hope to accomplish in the next five, ten, and twenty years? Where do you see your happiness? Where do you see your light? What successes do you want? What do you want to accomplish? As you think through these questions, what pictures come to mind? Dreams are fun to think about, but challenging to accomplish. The difference between those who live their dreams and those who don't is ambition and hard work. Remember, you already made the decision—now is the time to act!

EXERCISE

1. List the main things you would like to accomplish.
2. Next to the above list, break each goal down into one-, five-, ten-, and twenty-year goals. Write one, five, ten, or twenty beside each as the timeline for achieving that goal.
3. Think about the next twelve months and write out the steps you would need to take to:
    a. Accomplish one-year goals.
    b. Begin working on your five-year goals.
    c. Continue to plan your ten- and twenty-year goals.

Create a list based on the second question above. Save this list somewhere you can revisit it every year. One suggestion is revisiting your list in either December or January of every year so you can set intentions for the upcoming year based on these goals. Create a calendar reminder and have it repeat every year. Each year, look at that reminder with your goals incorporated in the description. Review what you have accomplished, and update what you would like to do the following year. Keep track of your successes so you can see how far you have come.

When you set goals, it is important to know that goals change. You do not want the same things today you wanted when you were five. Allow your goals to be fluid, but not forgotten. Allow them to shift with your shifting needs. Maintain your intention to continue to accomplish set goals. Keep the desire to continue to find happiness and light. Just like the light bulb continued to evolve, allow yourself to do the same. Along the way, you may set aside some goals. Others you will work diligently to achieve. You might hit your mark early, or you might get delayed. Either way, don't stop until you have accomplished the things you know will serve you and your life well. They will create happiness within and around you. Find the light!

EXPECTING CHANGE

You will change. Change is expected, and it is a necessary part of development, no matter what age you are. Don't get stagnant. Continue to learn. Continue to grow. As I said, the coping skills you used when you were five should not be the same skills you use today. This last activity will help you invest in future coping skills.

1. List a coping skill or skills you no longer need and describe why. Journal about new coping skills you could use that would be better suited for your current circumstances.

2. List three coping skills you can use on your journey that will drive you closer to success, happiness, and light.

3. Next, describe *why* you chose these three skills.

4. Finally, journal about the "how." How do you see these three coping skills brightening your path as you achieve your goals?

SUMMARY

Congratulations! You are well on your way to finding more peace among your pieces. We all have broken parts. What makes the biggest difference is what we choose to do with the pieces. If you decide to mend after hurt and find value in the pieces you carry, it will bring you light. I believe in you and in the pieces you carry. Though you may have scratches and scars, you are more valuable than you think. Taking the time to invest in yourself will create light in your life.

Believe in yourself as you believe in others. Give light to yourself just as you have given and shared your light with others. No one can get through life alone. Though at times being alone is valuable and necessary, don't live there. Don't live in the darkness. The light is waiting and wants to shine on you. Take advantage of this opportunity to truly invest in yourself.

Chapter 2

BECOMING FAMILIAR WITH YOUR STRENGTHS

"Genius is one percent inspiration and ninety-nine percent perspiration."

— Thomas Edison,
Inventor of the Phonograph

Just like the light bulb is one whole with separate parts, you are made up of distinct parts, each serving a specific purpose. The light bulb has an outer shell and filament, which is what Edison perfected to get the bulb to work properly. It also has the Edison Screw—the standard-sized socket fitting most US light bulbs. For the lights to come on, a whole system has to work—the socket that the bulb screws into, the light switch, and all the other components must work for the system to work effectively. Thus, the invention of the light bulb and the filament were not where the genius ended. The ideas needed to continue to expand, grow, and fit for the system to work. If one part did not align, the system would not produce light. This invention changed the way people lived because it was invested in and explored until it served the desired needs.

In the 1800s, with this new light in the world, people extended the day. More was accomplished after dark because of the light bulb; things that would not have been possible otherwise. Continuing to develop the light bulb and the infrastructure to deliver electricity made Edison's life better, but it also helped everyone in the world. Sometimes you don't see the effect your efforts have, either on you or others. If you continue to do your best, be kind, and stay ethical, you will make the world better for yourself and everyone around you.

The light bulb shines light and improves the world daily just by being itself and simply working. Today, it turns on and off when you flip the switch. People have improved it so it can do even more now. Dimmer switches allow you to control the brightness. You now have a lot of control over how much light the bulb produces, how much light you choose to have, and how much light you want to enjoy.

As you continue to strengthen your skills, you will be able to shine brighter in your own and others' lives. Someone may even say you spread light into their life by how you live. Inadvertently giving others the strength to light their own world and feel encouraged and inspired is a wonderful bonus feeling when you begin to shine. When you shine, you bring light into the world. You make the light in the world stronger. You brighten not only your own life, but also the lives of everyone around you.

AVOIDING THE DARKNESS

The opposite of light is darkness. The darkness is where negative self-talk lives. It is where the lies presented by your thoughts hide. The darkness tells you that you are not worthy. It tells us you that you cannot turn into reality your long-term dreams. Maybe it's telling you that you will never heal from the pain you carry. Worst of all, it could be telling you that if you share your light, you will have less light in your life. The darkness is never-ending and can seem like it's always there. The negative messages the darkness produces are endless.

The darkness is wrong.

Hope lives. Light brings light. Once you begin to really believe you are worthy of the light, you begin to realize strengthening yourself is something to be proud of. You grow in these moments, and the world gets brighter. Realize continuing to strive to become better adds light to the world. Everyone grows brighter. Your light is important and needed. Just like you have gleaned things from experiencing other people's light, so the world benefits from your brightly shining light.

The darkness will tell you light is limited, but that is not true. There is both unlimited darkness and unlimited light. What you choose to put into the world is what grows. If you put hate and disgust into the world, it will grow. If you put light and love into the world, it will grow. Do not believe the lie that sharing your light will diminish it. Anywhere light shines, darkness cannot survive.

Share your light!

Allow yourself to be vulnerable and share your light. The more light you share, the more it will grow in the world. And everyone knows the world can always use more light.

Fair warning—when you share your light, ensure you choose good people to support you. Unfortunately, darkness can seep in where it is not wanted. Your light is valuable and should be honored. Choose to share your light with those who will honor it and you without bringing the darkness in.

SETTING BOUNDARIES

When setting boundaries, leave them a bit more open to the people who accept you and love you when you are sad. Those who stick by you at your worst have depth and built trust. Anyone in your inner circle should support you, whether you are up or down. Your emotions are a rainbow with depth, and those who stand by you when you're having a bad day are your true lightkeepers.

This approach does not give anyone the green light to treat others disrespectfully. Do not tolerate abuse under any circumstances. Bad experiences in the past do not give others permission to mistreat you, nor do your difficulties give you that right toward others.

Some will use difficulties as an excuse to mistreat others. Oddly enough, some enjoy living in darkness and use stress, life transitions, grief, a bad day, getting fired, etc. to act out in inappropriate ways. Never use your rainbow of emotions to justify allowing your darkness to come out toward another.

The first step is to set appropriate boundaries to protect yourself. The second step is ensuring and growing your ability to address the darkness within when it tries to come out so you do not bleed darkness on others. Everyone carries some darkness. Darkness includes the things you struggle with, but darkness does not have to rule your life. When you find your internal light, you find the power, strength, optimism, and joy to shield yourself from the darkness.

Don't share your light with everyone you meet. Choose to share your light with others who are also light seekers. If you run into a light-sucker, sometimes no light can help them until they decide they are ready to live differently. Until then, your light could potentially be damaged as you hope your light will help them grow.

Stop shining your light on someone when you find they are a light-sucker. However, if you shine your light on someone and they abuse your trust, that says more about them than it does about you. Again: If you shine your light on someone you thought you could open up to, and they take advantage of your light, that says more about *them* than it does about *you*.

FINDING YOUR STRENGTHS

Think about someone you mistakenly chose to share your light with. Journal about the following:

1. How did you know they had been careless with the information/ feelings you shared with them?
2. How did you know they had been careless with the light you shared?
3. What in your gut told you to be careful the next time you chose to share something special with them?

Those answers are your strengths! Go back and read them. What you wrote will serve to help you understand, know, and be confident in choosing whom to share your light with. Invest in and trust your intuition.

Think about times when you did not follow your intuition, your gut—learn from them, and then set appropriate boundaries. Sharpen your skills in knowing whom to trust. This skill is a strength. Keep it with you. Sharpen it through ongoing experience.

Life is always giving us a chance to rebound when we mess up and trust someone we should not have trusted. Life gives us many chances to practice the skill of discernment. Learn from those mistakes. Have grace and forgiveness. Forgiving is not forgetting. It is letting go and removing another's power to control us and our thoughts. In forgiving, we learn something new about ourselves and we are presented with an opportunity—a new chance to set boundaries and protect our light. Set those boundaries and move forward.

EXERCISE

To fight against those who would bring darkness into your life, try this quick meditative practice:

1. Think of someone you are very fond of. Take a minute to really think about them. You should be feeling some warm fuzzies.
2. Think about them, and say, "I wish you well."
3. Say it in your mind five times.
4. Then think about someone you are *not* very fond of, someone who may bring darkness into your life.
5. Think about them, and say, "I wish you well."
6. Say it five times while thinking about them.

Starting this meditative exercise with someone you are fond of gives your brain some good feelings and preps your thoughts for the more challenging task of thinking that same thought, "I wish you well," about someone you are not very fond of. Fighting off the darkness can be exceedingly difficult at times, especially if you are unable to get away from the person who brings that darkness into your life. Use this exercise when they offend you, hurt you, and/or try to make the darkness stronger. Say to yourself, "I wish you well," and then move on. This might not be the easiest exercise, but it can give you the strength to help you fight off the darkness when your light seems dim.

SUMMARY

The darkness can be strong and feel overwhelming at times, but the light is always there. You may need someone to show you the spark because the darkness feels so heavy. Remember the strengths you carry with you as weapons to fight the darkness. Continue to make the effort to get stronger and add to your list of strengths. The journey can be long, but you will find sunshine in the least expected places. Continue to believe, do the work, and don't quit.

Chapter 3

ILLUMINATING YOUR DEVELOPMENT

"Let the future tell the truth and evaluate each one according to his work and accomplishments. The present is theirs, the future for which I really worked, is mine."

— Nikola Tesla,
Electrical Engineer, Inventor

Just like the light bulb went through different developmental stages, so will you. The light bulb was not invented on the first try, with the glass bulb, the filament, and the Edison Screw all working together correctly and cohesively. Rather, it had to undergo hundreds of evolutions to bring it to its intended bright future. You are the same. You were not born with the ability to walk, talk, and take care of yourself on your own, and to this day, there is still so much for you to learn. Never become stagnant. No matter your age, continue to grow and expand your abilities, knowledge, and experience. With intentional action comes growth, development, and a richness that will deepen your entire being.

STAGE 1: EXPLORING LIFE

Think about where you are now and where you have been. Key moments in your journey have changed your path. By being engaged, life came alongside you and aided your development. Maybe you took a chance on a new career, chose an unexpected path, or moved to a new state. The choices you made brought you to this very moment, reading this book, reflecting on your life and your future.

One of my key moments in exploring life came when I met my best friend. We were both in fifth grade and clicked instantly. I started spending a lot of time at her house. Her parents went to church every Sunday. My parents are not religious, but I started attending church with her and her family. Through our friendship, I learned a lot about religion and witnessed a different way of living. This experience would forever change me since I went on to attend a Bible college and later received my master's in marriage and family counseling. None of this would have happened if I were not open to exploring new friendships through my relationship with life. If not for this friendship, I would not be where I am today. I encourage you to explore life to the fullest. Engage in activities beyond your comfort zone because with that engagement, you learn and grow.

The way you choose to interact and engage with life will help shape your development and relationship with life. If you invest in life, life will also invest in you. If you choose to get bored and stagnant, life will also become boring. Do you find yourself with a lot of free time, and if so, how are you choosing to spend it? Do you then choose to learn something new? Do you choose to take a much-needed break and rest? Or are you wasting that free time and not really engaging?

STAGE 2: YOUR RELATIONSHIP WITH LIFE

Engaging in the adventure of life is like math. The more you learn about how to figure it out, the more confident and knowledgeable you become. The more comfortable and knowledgeable you become, the more success you experience. Failure is a natural part of development. To figure out math problems, you must try and fail, and then you learn. Learning to figure out life means trying, engaging, discovering, and then you will see growth. Hang on to failure. Failures are learning experiences where you find what does not work—just like Edison. He learned many ways that did not work, and each time he put that information in his pocket, improved his design, and moved on. He did not dwell on the failed attempts. He probably experienced disappointment, but in the end, every time he failed, he learned and went on to create one of the most useful tools in the world. You will have ups and downs in your development, bumps in the road—it is all part of the process. Trust the process. Your journey has purpose!

Reflect on your journey up to this moment. You have experienced celebrations, losses, welcomed transitions, regret, and events that did not go your way. Each experience brings up different emotions. Those experiences are part of your foundation and have helped shape the person you are today. You can look back at those experiences and draw strength from the positive memories as well as insight from the painful memories. This is the rainbow of emotions, and without these experiences, you would not be as insightful, empathetic, aware, and intelligent. Your history shapes your future. Reflect on the past. Engage with the present. Prepare for the future. You are now in a relationship with life.

STAGE 3: YOU ARE THE LIGHT BULB

The next stage in your development is realizing you are the light bulb. You are a whole, valuable being with an intentional purpose. Some get stuck in this stage, never moving on because they don't realize what they have to offer the world is both important and needed. To be your best, you need to recognize your own value. This can feel difficult and uncomfortably vulnerable. One way to practice recognizing your value is to set aside space a couple of times a week to review your strengths. Think about the things you bring to the world that help it shine brighter. Your worth is there—it just may be a bit dim. Not to worry; as you continue your journey, you will find it.

If you do not struggle in this area—way to go! You have put in some good self-reflection work, and it is one of your strengths. For those who do struggle with finding their worth, and those who are already aware of their value—a good activity is to list your strengths on note cards and go through them when you have a bad day. Everyone gets down at some point. Activities like these remind you of your value and strengths and are a good way to engage the light and fight off the darkness.

STAGE 4: THE LIGHT WITHIN

Investing in your light is the best way to remain engaged in life and fight off the darkness. Self-care is another great way to invest in your light. You can practice things like getting enough sleep, eating healthily, ensuring you get exercise and fresh air, spending time with people who build you up, and taking time to be with yourself. Take a moment to write down five things you will do to invest in yourself over the next month.

Next, open your calendar and take hold of your future. Schedule appointments to engage in the five activities you listed. Think of these activities as your "dates with life." You are now in a relationship with life, and something you do in a relationship is invest time, effort, and intentionality. Make it a self-care habit. Plan one "date with life" every month. These dates can be with yourself or another person, but the focus is on investing in yourself and your relationship with life.

STAGE 5: THE LIGHT IN OTHERS

Your light is getting brighter, and it's time to realize you also have light to give others. Your illumination offers hope to those around you. The interesting thing is you don't know who you inspire by just being yourself and making the choices you make. Humans are natural observers, and we learn from those around us. You learn a lot about what you want to do and what you want to avoid by watching how other people live. The same is true of the people around you. Your light could encourage others without you even knowing it. Kindness, compassion, and empathy, to name a few, are acts that brighten people's day. You never know what others are struggling with. If you can be a light in someone's world just by being authentic, kind, and considerate, you will make the world brighter by sharing your inner light.

STAGE 6: NEVER STOP LEARNING

Your journey does not stop at realizing you are a valuable entity with insight to offer the world. Be on the lookout for opportunities to continue growing through expanding your experiences and knowledge. When you are most engaged, you will find yourself gaining depth of thought and ability. Learning takes many paths, but I encourage you to embrace experiences you would not normally be drawn to.

In the counseling world, focal conflict theory is based on the premise that you learn when your anxiety rises just a bit. Anxiety is an odd emotion because when most people feel it, they tend to see it as a negative emotion. I want to challenge the way you look at anxiety. When you experience a low level of anxiety, you have an opportunity to learn and grow. Just because an emotion feels bad does not mean it is bad for you. Anxiety has a purpose. If you can reframe low-level anxiety, instead of it creating stress, it could begin to create growth. When anxiety shows up, ask it what it wants from you. What is it trying to teach you? It may have a hidden and healthy purpose.

When our system is out of balance, it can elevate anxiety, and that is a whole different topic. If you find yourself becoming overly anxious, like so many people do, there are ways to help reduce the anxiety. Reach out to your doctor, counselor, holistic healer…whomever you trust to work through whatever is causing you increased anxiety. I've been there and understand it can be a difficult journey, but don't give up because light could be just around the corner!

STAGE 7: LIFE IS FRAGILE

Being made of delicate glass, the light bulb is fragile. Life is also fragile. Realizing life is fragile is the next stage in the developmental process of *The Light Bulb Effect*. When my daughter was born, I laughed at some of the thoughts I was having—one of which was being confused about why we are born with an endoskeleton instead of an exoskeleton. Ants have an exoskeleton (an external skeleton) that supports and protects their body, but my new baby girl was all soft and mushy with her skeleton on the inside. I knew life was fragile, but before I had my daughter, I hadn't realized just how exposed and fragile we really are. I constantly thought about how to protect her physically, emotionally, and in all the other ways a parent is supposed to protect. Realizing life is fragile puts a certain emphasis on the effort you make to take care of yourself and those around you. If you have ever experienced loss, grief, or even an accident that changed you or someone you know, you realize at any moment this fragile life can be altered forever.

STAGE 8: CARING FOR YOURSELF AND OTHERS

The eighth stage of development in *The Light Bulb Effect* is understanding how to invest in caring for yourself and others. This is an essential part of a healthy and balanced life. How you choose to invest in yourself and others is incredibly important. As a therapist working with couples, I talk to them about the importance of creating a regular date night. The investment of time and experience helps keep people's connection strong. This is true in relationships with partners, friends, children, or even those you lead. The investment of time, energy, experience, and intentionality makes people feel special and cared for. This investment pays off for you and all those around you.

STAGE 9: KNOWING WHAT TO DO WHEN YOU BURN OUT

Finally, knowing what to do when you burn out is important. All light bulbs that burn long enough burn out. You understand the value of getting enough sleep, eating healthy foods, exercising, making connections, and so on.... But the question is: What if you're doing all those things and you still burn out? At some point, you will experience burnout. The trick to getting through that stage more easily is to have skills in place that you can use to recharge your battery.

Imagine that you have been playing Halo on Xbox and the aliens have swarmed you. You might have all the skills in the world, but if there are too many aliens, they are going to drain your power. Imagine those aliens are your daily tasks. You can manage a lot of things daily; you already do. But when you are surrounded by aliens (daily tasks), each can drain your energy until you are exhausted. Just like planning intentional dates or time to spend with those around you whom you connect with, you should also plan intentional times to recharge your battery to ensure you do your best to avoid burnout.

While reading this chapter, you wrote a list of five things you can do to invest in yourself over the next month. Take a moment to reflect on those five things and commit to at least three of them. Then commit to completing the other two the following month. Let this become a habit. Work on realizing that investing in yourself and your well-being is just as important as investing in those around you.

SUMMARY

Your metaphorical light bulb will experience nine developmental stages. Each stage will teach you something and provide an experience. Don't let anxiety about the unknown stifle your development. Begin to challenge yourself to embrace small doses of anxiety. Acknowledge the anxiety that comes with trying something new, and realize it is there to help you get through the situation, to learn, and grow. Each stage is valuable and important. Take time to sit with each new experience because each one has something to teach you to help prepare you for the next chapter of your life.

It is important to note that, though these are stages, you may go through the stages at various times and not in order. It is okay to jump around throughout the nine stages of development. Just continue to engage, experience, learn, and grow. You've got this!

Chapter 4

DISCOVERING YOUR AUTHENTIC SELF

"One of the greatest discoveries a person makes, one of their great surprises, is to find they can do what they were afraid they couldn't do."

— Henry Ford,
American Industrialist

Have you ever felt you were investing time in several different worlds, like you have things you like that conflict with each other? Maybe you experience conflicting emotions over various situations. This can be confusing, but as you grow and mature, so does your authentic self. You will experience in-depth emotional responses to situations, and those emotions may seem confusing in the beginning. Realize the authentic self, as it matures, can hold more than one emotion at a time, and some of those emotions can appear to conflict with one another. The truth is the emotions may be complimentary. Taking a deep look within can bring up a range of emotions from joy and happiness to fear and doubt. Discovering their authentic self sometimes excites people, but others become anxious and feel exposed.

If you had the pleasure of watching Disney's *Inside Out*, you know the main character, Riley, is struggling with growing older and moving. As you watch, the characters representing her emotions—Sadness, Joy, Disgust, and Anger—are trying to maintain Riley's well-being. Joy, the main character of Riley's emotions, tries to maintain happiness. Sadness tries to creep in, and Joy tries to keep Sadness busy with tasks such as reading manuals. Joy doesn't realize until the end that events in Riley's life are so much richer when both Sadness and Joy work together. Joy realizes having multiple emotions in any given moment helps give life depth.

LIVING IN THE LIGHT

Just like the light bulb can have many distinct colors, you have many distinct emotions and experiences. At one time, I really struggled with the different "worlds" I was involved in, but at the same time, I was unwilling to sacrifice one for the other. After a lot of reflection, I decided I did not need to choose—I could keep both worlds, even though from the outside they seemed to conflict. They involved my faith in God and my participation in the Burning Man community. If you don't know about the Burning Man community, in short, it is a cultural movement that focuses on art and experience, culminating in an annual event in Nevada around the end of August. Looking in from the outside, Christians can appear very judgmental and rigid. Looking in from the outside, Burning Man can appear very atheistic. Yet when both of these worlds are combined, taking the good from each one is like experiencing what Joy and Sadness realized. When you allow yourself to experience the richness in life through experience, there will always be things to leave behind, but there will also be light found in unexpected environments that will help you grow.

While attending a women's group, I realized I could continue to participate in both worlds. In the group, I talked about struggling with the feeling I was involved in two different worlds. I shared how both worlds were especially important to me, and I didn't want to have to choose between them. The meeting leader retrieved a small marble resembling a globe from her bag and handed it to me. She said she had been given the marble years earlier and had carried it with her ever since. As she handed me this little marble of the world, she offered encouragement, telling me I did not have to choose, that we can participate in multiple "worlds." Looking around the room, I saw people accepting both my faith in God and my participation in the Burning Man community. From that day forward, I carried that marble with me everywhere until a couple of years later when fate brought me to another friend who was having a similar struggle. I reached into my bag, pulled out the marble, and passed it to my friend while offering words of encouragement, saying they did not have to choose between worlds.

While exploring your authentic self, areas of your life may seem to conflict, and you may think you have to choose between them—but don't feel trapped. Take an in-depth look and ask yourself, "Who says I must choose?" Is it the culture you live in or is it a boundary you need to set for yourself to be healthy? When you are presented with a self-reflective opportunity like this, it can be the best time to really take a deeper look at who you are authentically and ask yourself some tough questions.

EXERCISE

1. What five words would you use to describe who you are at your core?

2. As you reflect on the words above, do you feel you hide any of those elements from the world?
3. Are any of the elements listed above things you want to shine more light on and share with the world?

LETTING GO OF THE FEAR

Fear can make it difficult to show the world your authentic self. We tend to show the world what we think it will accept. We may be afraid of others judging us. I know I was. As I continued through my "thought journey," trying to reconcile my two worlds, a phrase kept coming to mind: "What people choose to see in me teaches me a lot about them." Who you are is who you are, and what others think of you says nothing about you. Continue to choose your authentic self. Start to show people your authentic self. Don't be surprised if some are wary of parts of you they have not previously seen, but know it is time to get out of the dark. It is time to choose you. If some people decide they no longer want to invest time in you, that says more about them.

Peer feedback is part of helping your authentic self grow stronger. Be open to feedback from the people you trust because that feedback can be especially important. Be wary of the people who give feedback before earning your trust. I am open to hearing feedback from anyone. I look at it as an opportunity for self-reflection. When presented with feedback from a friend or enemy, I ask myself the following questions:

1. Is this feedback helpful?
2. Is this feedback coming from a place of love?

3. Is this person pointing out a problem I really do need to address?

The reason I encourage asking yourself these questions is because if someone takes the time to point out something they see, it is worth taking sixty seconds to think about it. You may find value. *But* remember the feedback may not be an accurate picture of who you are. If so, let that feedback go. Evaluating yourself and the person giving the feedback is an important part of the process of growth. In the end, whether you accept the feedback is up to you.

OPENING UP YOUR HEART

The filament is at the heart of the light bulb. It is designed to create the light the rest of the bulb supports. Your authentic self is at the heart of who you are. It is designed to create the light the rest of your being supports. Your authentic self is comprised of dozens of elements that make up who you are and who you continue to become.

As you work toward strengthening your authentic self, it will become noticeably easier to open your heart to new experiences. This has a cyclical effect. You take a chance and show your authentic self to the world; the world accepts what you present. In turn, you grow stronger and show more of yourself, which the world, again, accepts. Don't let bumps or grumps stop you from being openly genuine.

Through this process of trial and error, assessing whom you can open up to and who might be challenging, you will learn. Just because someone does not like something you are showing them, does not mean you have to change. It goes back to ensuring you evaluate their feedback and *deciding for yourself* if it is helpful. Helpful feedback will help you grow. Unhelpful feedback lets you practice setting boundaries, and you may realize they are not in line with your growth goals. Through this process, you will learn and open your heart to feedback, to growing, and to becoming more of your authentic self—both the good and the bad help you on your journey of discovery.

Exploring your authenticity can bring up feelings of vulnerability, especially in the face of fear, mistrust, pain, and uncertainty. In experiencing your vulnerability, you will grow the most. In your vulnerability, you have the greatest chance of getting hurt. At this point in the process, after one or two hurts, many people give up and expect that to always be the pattern. Just like Edison, now is *not* the time to give up. Now is the time to reflect on the pain, learn, and grow. It is time to remain optimistic.

You may encounter those with selfish intentions. When and if you get caught in someone's web, give yourself grace and get out of the situation as soon as possible. Just because one person misuses your vulnerability does not mean the next person will. Take heart in knowing you will get better at spotting red flags.

Opening your heart to experience and growing your authentic self is not a journey for the weak. It is paved with hurt, but you will also find the most rewarding relationships along the way. As you get more comfortable with showing people who you really are, you will find yourself experiencing deeper friendships, swimming in deeper levels of trust, and participating in genuine interactions. That happens because you have taken the scary step of showing the world who you really are, and because of that, you will begin to attract people who are doing the same. It is the best feeling in the world to sit with someone and know they know your deepest secrets and still love you. When you open your heart and show the world your authentic self, you will experience the greatest forms of acceptance. It may take a while, sometimes even years. Remember, this is a journey. Invest the time and effort into yourself and you will notice the people around you will start to change as well. It is a very rewarding journey, with ups, downs, and all arounds. Though the journey is not always easy, it's worth it!

EXERCISE

1. Are you hiding parts of yourself in the dark that you would like to shine light on?
2. If you answered yes to the above question, list up to three people you feel would protect your story if you shared it with them.

CHALLENGE

Think about contacting the people you listed above to share your story. Set a time to go out for lunch and connect with them. Take a chance with your authenticity. Be vulnerable. See how it goes. Remember, if they do not respond as you hope, it's okay. They might not be ready. But taking a chance to create and deepen your connection is more about the journey you are taking no matter how it goes—you are creating space for yourself to grow. Good luck!

SUMMARY

Discovering your authentic self is remarkably like the journey a light bulb takes. You start out whole, but get some scratches, bumps, and bruises, and may even break along the way. But there is so much beauty in your pieces! And on top of that, the world is a better place when you share some of that brokenness to build positive connections. Not only does the world benefit from your authentic self, but you will find yourself making deeper connections, and your life will change for the better by being vulnerable with others. Remember to be choosy about whom you share your vulnerability and authentic self with. Surround yourself with people you trust to share your story. Your story is sacred, just like theirs, and not everyone will get the opportunity to hear it. But whomever you choose to share it with will be better for hearing it, and you will be better for sharing it. Your connection will be better. This is where life becomes richer and brighter.

Section 2

DEFINING THE PIECES OF THE LIGHT BULB

"The dark does not destroy the light; it defines it. It's our fear of the dark that casts our joy into the shadows."

— Brené Brown,
The Gifts of Imperfection

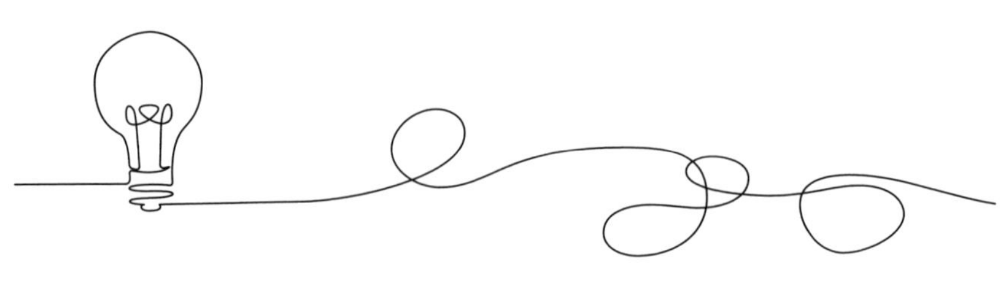

Chapter 5

INVESTING IN YOUR LIGHT

"You get the best out of others when you give the best of yourself."

— Harvey Samuel Firestone,
Founder of Firestone Tire and Rubber and
Friend of Thomas Edison

Have you felt so burned out that you could spend a week in bed and still not catch up on rest? If so, you are not alone. You may go through life with a task list, schedule, and probably some idea of what the next day, week, and month will look like. Life can get overwhelming and make you feel like you can't keep your head above water. Times like these can create stress, anxiety, and a sense of struggle. It may feel like the tasks the world is asking of you have no end. To keep your light bright, you must invest in self-care. Just like the light bulb draws its strength from an energy source, you need a power source to draw energy from so you can stay charged and ready for what life brings your way.

Self-care is often discussed and encouraged in the helping professions because it helps maintain personal strength and well-being while serving others. Self-care is not only beneficial for professionals but everyone everywhere. Without taking time to invest in and care for yourself, you run the risk of burnout. Self-care comes in many forms, from ensuring you get enough sleep to eating healthy foods and choosing healthy people to have in your life. It could also take the form of self-date nights—setting aside time for rest or taking yourself on an adventure.

THE SELF-CARE EXPERIENCE

Introverts and extroverts experience self-care differently. They get recharged differently. Introverts recharge by spending time alone. Extroverts recharge around other people. The concept of someone being an extrovert or introvert is interesting because everyone is some degree of both. You might find you are an extroverted introvert—you recharge when you are alone, but you could be the life of the party when you are with others. On the opposite side, if you are an introverted extrovert, you could find yourself recharging when you are quietly sitting with people.

Understanding how you relate to these concepts and how you recharge is an important step to healthy self-care. Understanding how you recharge will help you begin choosing the activities and methods you will use to recharge.

To determine whether you are an introvert or extrovert, ask yourself:

1. Do I feel drained or energized after being with people?
2. Do I feel drained or energized after being alone?

The answers will tell you if you recharge your light when you are alone or when you are with people. Next, answer the following question to determine if you might be an extroverted-introvert or the opposite:

1. When I am with people, do I enjoy being in front of the group or in the background?

Introvert	Extrovert
If you ***do*** feel drained after being with people and you do ***not*** like being in front of the group, you are an Introvert. You recharge your light alone and probably feel drained after being with people for an extended period.	If you do ***not*** feel drained after being with people, feeling recharged instead, ***and*** you like being in the front of the group, you are an Extrovert. You recharge your light when you're with multiple people and feel drained if you are alone for an extended period.
Extroverted-Introvert	**Introverted-Extrovert**
If you ***do*** feel drained after being with people and also ***like*** being in front of the group when you are with people, you are an Extroverted-Introvert. You recharge your light alone, but you also enjoy being with people and at the front of the group for short periods.	If you do ***not*** feel drained after being with people and, in fact, feel recharged, ***but*** you do ***not*** like being at the front of the group, you are an Introverted-Extrovert. You recharge your light with people, but you do not really enjoy being at the front of the group.

The thing to remember as you find your quadrant is everyone enjoys both to some extent: being with people *and* being alone at times. Determining if you are an Introvert or Extrovert is more about *where* you get your light recharged. As Harvey Samuel Firestone said, “You get the best out of others when you give the best of yourself.” Knowing how to recharge your light is the foundation to ensuring you have the energy to give the best of yourself to others.

ENJOYING SOLITUDE

Now that we have established everyone needs a bit of both solitude and company, let’s dive into ways to recharge in solitude. The ability to spend time alone is useful in becoming a whole person. You need to strengthen all your parts, and being comfortable alone is no exception. This will come easy for introverts. Extroverts may struggle to figure out what to do during alone time until they establish the habit. Look at spending time alone, with just yourself, as one of the many healthy habits necessary for a well-rounded life.

How do you do this? Start by scheduling a self-date night once a month. You could start with just thirty minutes, an hour, or even longer if this comes easy for you. Be intentional by putting it in your calendar as an appointment so you know you have plans with yourself to recharge your light. Of course, you can move it around for events, but if you move the appointment, don’t cancel it—instead, move it to a different time. Try not to get into the habit of moving the appointment around because the whole point in forming this habit is to make yourself a priority.

I practice this habit and make a point to schedule time. Occasionally, when friends ask me to go out and I already have self-date time scheduled, I just say I already have plans. “I am so sorry, but I have put aside some time for myself that night to recharge. I would love to do something with you soon. Is there another time we could get together?” No one has ever gotten upset when I told them this. It’s important to tell your friend you want to spend time with them and ask when you could make that happen. Don’t leave this part out. A friend wanting to spend time with you is a sacred thing. This approach protects the times I set aside to recharge and also lets my friends know they are important and I want to spend time with them soon.

If you are new to dating yourself, you can try some of these approaches. Plan the time, place, meal, and activity. Take yourself on a hike or go to a movie. I have planned special meals at home, with the activities including picking up the groceries for the meal, lighting a candle, turning on some music, and just spending time in the kitchen making a gourmet meal. I have also chosen to order food, rent a movie, or have a home spa day. Think of the things you really enjoy doing, and then turn those things into a self-date and invest time in your own well-being. Remember, this practice is important for introverts *and* extroverts. In the quiet moments with myself, I have the best ideas and get the most rest to help me get ready for the world.

INVESTING IN CONNECTION

The opposite side of needing solitude is needing company. Investing only in solitude is not effective unless you also invest in company and connection. For extroverts, this will come easy—introverts are probably feeling a bit apprehensive right now. Having a support system is vital to getting through life's ups and downs. The best way to create and maintain a healthy support system is to invest in the people who invest in you. Invest in those who have shown they can be trusted. In a perfect world, your support system would be made up of family, friends, mentors, and coworkers. Not everyone has those connections. But it's important to understand you can create a future different from your past. You can create your own positive support system among the people who have earned a place in your life by their actions, how they treat you, and how they treat the things you care about. Choose wisely, and set boundaries as needed when you get new information.

Making and creating connections requires the same intentionality as planning time for solitude. A past mentor once told me you buy memories. At the time, we were coworkers taking a group of high school students to Great America. My mentor's daughter was on the trip, and she asked me to go on a giant (and to me, scary) ride that required buying a ticket. Not only do I not like heights, but as a poor college student, I was tight on money. My mentor offered to pay, saying, "You buy memories." I thought, *Okay, I am here to make positive connections with these students, and I hope I don't die*. I went on the ride, and to this day, I remember it fondly. As a mother, I have taken that advice to heart. These intentional actions make memories, and more importantly, make connections.

Memories and connections are not always about actually buying something. The concept of "buying memories" is more about the intention behind the action. You don't have to buy memories; you just need to intentionally plan, follow through, and be present to make memories.

To create and deepen connections, you need intention, but it doesn't stop there. Good intentions without follow through lead nowhere. Intentionality (thoughts) must be connected to following through (action) to build connection and community. Good intentions without follow through are pointless. If you have both intention and follow through, you will start to see your connections and community grow. You can build connections and community for free—hike, walk, go to the park. Just ensure you have positive intentions and follow through.

When people understand you care about the things they care about, they feel loved. In those actions, connections are made and buckets get filled. Everyone has an invisible bucket needing to be filled. If you have had the pleasure of reading the children's book, *Have You Filled a Bucket Today?*, you know about this concept. In the book, author Carol McCloud eloquently describes how everyone has an invisible bucket they carry with them. When the bucket is full, they feel happy, and when the bucket is empty, they feel sad. Buckets are filled by sharing love and kindness.

SUMMARY

Now that you understand which of the four quadrants you land in, you can more easily identify the activities that will keep your inner light charged. Remember, extrovert or introvert, you will benefit from putting effort into both solitude and connection. Intention is amazing, but without follow through, it has no benefit. Also remember to schedule time with both yourself and those you know will fill your bucket. Activities do not have to cost money. Get creative with planning intentional time with yourself and people in your support network. You buy memories not only with money, but with time. Both are equally rewarding if the connection, intentionality, follow through, and recharge are happening. This is a journey, not a sprint, and you are doing amazingly well!

Chapter 6

EMBRACING THE BROKEN PIECES

"In the position of an impartial student and observer I have sought less to indicate defects than to exhibit accomplishments."

— William E. Sawyer,
New York, January 15, 1881. *Electric Lighting By Incandescence, and Its Application to Interior Illumination: A Practice Treatise*

The pieces of your broken light bulb are beautiful. Your hardships may have left you with scratches, scars, and even broken pieces, but it's time to embrace the brokenness. You started out whole, but through life's experiences, choices, and events, you may now feel broken. As William E. Sawyer said, focus on the accomplishments, not the defects. So often, you are confronted with negative self-talk. Negative self-talk can feel a lot louder than the positive. It is time to choose to lower the volume on the negative, embrace the pieces, and in so doing, raise the volume on your positive self-talk.

Negative self-talk is the recitation of negative thoughts and beliefs you think and believe about yourself. It can attack how you do things, the way you look, the accomplishments you have yet to achieve, etc. Most of these beliefs you hold about yourself are inaccurate. In your thought life, they can sound overly critical. Negative self-talk tends to be critical, hurtful, damaging, and exceedingly difficult to let go of.

On the opposite side is positive self-talk. Positive self-talk recites the positive statements you tell yourself and believe. Take time to think about and build positive self-talk. It can take some time to develop it. You may not even realize some of the positive beliefs you hold. Through this self-reflective process, you will uncover more of your positive self-beliefs and thoughts and rein in negative beliefs.

EXERCISE

Think back to your very first memory. Was it happy, or does it carry some pain? Do you have a belief about yourself you carry with you from that first memory? The things you tell yourself are a direct reflection of the events you have experienced. Some events may have left behind some negative beliefs about yourself based on how people treated you or the choices you made. The amazing thing about doing self-talk work is there is always room for change and growth.

THINGS THAT BREAK YOU

It is no surprise the things that break people come from both internal and external sources. Hurt can also come through unfortunate natural circumstances and unforeseen accidents. You will find no shortage of hurt and loss in the world. What matters to your thought life is how you process each event. Be intentionally aware of the beliefs you adopt as you go through events that could break you into pieces. Choose which beliefs you will hold on to, keeping only those that will help you through similar circumstances.

If you have been alive long enough, you have experienced things that could break you—the loss of a loved one, divorce, an accident, an affair, money troubles, loss of a dream, etc. Whenever I give a speech about being broken, as I look around the room, I see people nodding in agreement, showing they can relate to loss. No one is alone in feeling broken. No one is untouched by the hurts that come with living. The unfortunate reality of life is everyone will experience pain, loss, and difficult transitions at one point or another.

Having gone through the pain of divorce, I can assure you I know your value does not decrease because of the broken pieces you carry. The absolute truth is we are all broken, trying to find wholeness. When we confront our broken pieces and learn to be more genuine with those around us, we build authenticity and can begin to heal.

THINGS THAT HEAL YOU

An odd but happy fact about embracing the pieces is when you do it once, it will be easier to do again. Embracing the broken pieces, increasing your positive self-talk, and finding community and connection to people who genuinely support you will lead to healing. It is so similar to Brené Brown's approach of shining light on the things life tells you that you should be ashamed of. When light is shined on those things, they lose their power. Light can penetrate the darkness, but the darkness cannot penetrate the light. When you learn to embrace your brokenness, you will find your hidden strengths waiting for you.

ACTIVITY # 1: STRENGTHENING YOUR INTERNAL LIGHT

1. Think about the positive side of who you are.
2. Purchase a set of three-by-five notecards and cut them in half. Find a place by your desk or nightstand where you can store these along with a pen.
3. As you think of positive self-talk statements, write them down on these notecards.
4. Review the cards often and add to them as positive self-beliefs come to you.

Do this activity each time you think of a positive statement about yourself. Review the cards every time negative self-talk tries to make you believe you are someone other than who you are. The more you do this, the more you train your brain to listen to the positive.

ACTIVITY #2: INCREASING YOUR EXTERNAL LIGHT

Make a list of five people you can trust. Begin to build and strengthen your relationship with these individuals by intentionally investing in them and their lives. They will become your team of cheerleaders made up of family and/or close friends. Investing in them is also an investment in yourself. Do things for them to let them know you care and can be there for them authentically.

A simple thing you can do is put their birthday on your calendar and send them a text on their special day. Allowing yourself to be authentic with them in both their joys and struggles helps provide good connection. This tells them they can do the same for you. When one of your people is struggling, reach out and ask if you can do anything for them. Authentic and genuine relationships are not formed by happenstance; they come from diligent investment, intention, and most importantly, follow through. This is your team, and you are a part of their team. Support each other in the good times and the bad. They will be your light when your light is dim. You will be their light when their light is dim. You will find strength in sharing your light with your team.

THE WAYS YOU BREAK

You can break in many ways. Your power is found in how you respond. We sometimes hear, "No one can make you feel something." This implies you choose your emotions and response to each situation. Quite the opposite is true. You are designed with a rainbow of emotions that naturally come out in various situations. For example, if someone lies to you, you feel betrayed. If someone does something behind your back, you will feel hurt and angry. Your emotions are indicators of something your body and your mind are telling you, to help you learn, get through the situation, and avoid similar situations in the future.

You will feel broken in many ways throughout life. The key to moving on successfully is ensuring your mental, emotional, and physical systems are working collaboratively for the overall benefit of your health. Listen to the feedback these three systems offer and make decisions based on this feedback. Each time you get this feedback, sit with it, reflect on it, ask what the system is trying to communicate, and then act accordingly.

One of the most productive actions you can take to live life to the fullest is to learn what you like and what you don't like. Next, seek the positive and decrease the negative. Set boundaries around things that break you. This can feel empowering, and alternately, feel intimidating. The ways you break and the things that break you will not produce happiness. You are the driver of your life, and you get to decide what you bring in and what you leave behind.

SETTING BOUNDARIES

Understanding the ways you break can help you see where setting boundaries will be helpful. In college, I worked the front desk at a hotel and often got off late. I'd be really tired the next day. On the weekend, I caught up on sleep as much as I could. I am a *big* believer in getting enough sleep to be fully engaged. Every Saturday, I intentionally turned off my alarm and let my body decide when I should wake. Then someone in my life started calling me early every Saturday morning.

I explained my situation and said I really needed to catch up on sleep on Saturday mornings. I asked them to call later, but they kept calling early every Saturday. Once I realized they were not going to respect this boundary, I started turning off my phone's ringer when I went to bed.

This really wasn't much of a disturbance, but it's an example of setting boundaries and how they can be reinforced when they are ignored. I learned at times I may have to take additional steps to enforce the needed action so I can maintain a healthy lifestyle.

You too can make requests and set boundaries in this way. Start by stating your boundary. If the person or people do not respect your request, think about steps you can take to ensure you are getting what you need. It could be turning off your ringer at night, or something more serious like ending a relationship, or financially cutting off someone. Whatever boundary you are thinking about, remember you may need a plan B if the person or people do not respect your initial request.

You may feel guilty about setting boundaries, but they protect you from things that may break you. Understand that if you do not advocate for yourself, no one else is going to. Self-advocacy is the only way to get what you need, and if you do not enforce and reinforce your needs, the door is open for others to decide how to treat you. Do not allow yourself to break for the benefit or comfort of another. You may believe you are making their situation easier or more comfortable, but you are taking away the authentic experience you share and sacrificing yourself in the process. You don't want to spend time with people who have you walking on eggshells. If you can't be your true self with another, they should not be in your inner circle.

As a therapist, I see this hesitancy to set boundaries the most when someone is in a relationship with a narcissist. You set a boundary because you know you need it to avoid being hurt. If someone ignores your boundaries, they do not respect you, and you should reconsider your relationship with them.

EMBRACING THE PIECES

Light can be gained through embracing the pieces of your brokenness. By taking an honest look at your brokenness, you can start to find healing. Seeing where life has not only broken you but also where life has offered healing is encouraging. Life will not leave you alone. Healing will always be in your journey. If you are having a tough time finding it right now, that's okay. Sometimes it may even be hard to trust that healing will come at all. That's okay too. It is normal to have doubts. This is why you lean on and reach out to the five people you thought about in activity two. When you cannot seem to find hope, those five people may be able to carry it for you.

Think about the things that brought light into your brokenness. Reflecting on the light that life has brought is an important part of recognizing that, though you've had to survive some tricky situations, life has not left you alone. Light could come in the form of the people around you or even in the comfort of a pet. The light is there to be found. It is okay if it is difficult to see right now; just don't give up. You have made it this far. You are fighting the good fight. Continue to lean on the things that give you strength and reach out to those who genuinely support and care for you.

SUMMARY

Beauty is found in your brokenness. Strength is found in your efforts. Life will not leave you alone if you continue to engage. Know whatever you are going through or have had to endure, it is only a chapter of your life, and a new chapter is just around the corner. You have the power within to change your future, not only for yourself, but for generations to come.

Life is full of struggles and broken pieces, but also hope and love. Keep looking for the things that make you happy. Continue to create and build genuine connections with people. Finally, continue to set boundaries with those who may create more broken pieces in your life. As always, make good choices for yourself and for those around you. You really can do this!

Chapter 7

CREATING ROOM FOR GROWTH

"A somebody was once a nobody who wanted to and did."

— John Burroughs,
American Naturalist

Have you ever had a light bulb burn out and thought to yourself, *I will get to that later*, and then later was not just a day or two but several weeks? Yeah, me too. This delay reflects some positive characteristics about how you approach life and growth. Think about the benefits of waiting to change a burned-out light bulb. It could mean at the time you did not *need* the light, and you chose to prioritize other, more urgent tasks. On the opposite side, it could also mean you needed a bit more rest and were waiting until you have more time on your hands. That light bulb eventually got changed when you needed the light most or when you found the time to do it. Whatever your reason, you understood the burned-out bulb would not get changed until you *wanted* to do it.

CREATING CHANGE

Finding the motivation to make the changes you know will help you lead a happy and healthy life can sometimes be difficult, but you have it in you. Finding the desire, wanting to make the change, and following through is a continuous journey that I encourage you to look at as an element of positive, habit-forming behavior. Positive habit-forming behavior is not a discipline that happens overnight; it is something to begin working on, practicing, and forming as part of your overall approach to life. Each decision you are confronted with, whether small or large, either strengthens your positive habit-forming behavior or strengthens your negative habit-forming behavior.

An example of a positive habit-forming behavior is choosing to drink water instead of soda when you really love to drink soda. Every time you choose to drink water, you strengthen your positive habit-forming behavior, and this informs and strengthens your resolve when you are presented with other choices. As you continue to make positive, healthy choices, you find it becoming easier to make more positive, healthy choices. This is not to say you will not be tempted and sometimes grab the metaphorical soda. You will. When that happens, give yourself grace and know sodas are an okay choice some of the time. In the long run, water is healthier.

When my son was born, I found myself craving these delicious cheesy breadsticks from Arctic Circle. When I got them, the cashier would ask if I wanted ranch or marinara. I fully understood the breadsticks were unhealthy enough on their own, but I really wanted the ranch. In the beginning, I was highly tempted to get the ranch, but I told myself if I was going to treat myself with breadsticks, I would make the healthier choice by opting for the marinara sauce. After getting the marinara sauce several times, I no longer wanted the ranch. This is an example of strengthening positive habit-forming behavior.

Where can you start choosing marinara instead of ranch? Where are you making an unhealthy choice that could be easily replaced with a healthier choice? Journal some thoughts about this concept as it applies to you. Choose one area where you could substitute marinara for ranch. This is how you begin and continue to create change—in the little decisions that end up adding up to big decisions.

John Burroughs' quote, "A somebody was once a nobody who wanted to and did," rings true in this section. If you want to, and you go after it, and you do it, you will have done it! Sometimes I find the things I go after are not the right path for me. Like Edison with the light bulb, I figure I tried and learned a lot more about myself—so I don't consider them a failure. If you go after something and find it is not the right path for you, congratulations! You did not fail. You learned more about yourself and how you interact with life. In these moments, some quit. Do *not* quit. These moments are only part of your journey. They are not the end of your journey. They are just as important as the "wins" because the difficult moments teach you and guide your path as much as the wins and will continue to do so.

EXERCISE

1. In which three areas can you start choosing marinara instead of ranch?

2. Now that you have identified three areas in which you can start working on strengthening positive habit-forming behavior, decide *how* you will choose marina instead of ranch.
3. What is your plan for making healthier choices when it comes to the three items you listed above?

CREATING ROOM

Since you now have a tool in your toolbelt for beginning to create change through positive habit-forming actions, let's discuss how to create room for growth. The first step in creating room to grow is realizing it will not be there until you genuinely want to change. Occasionally, people get caught in their dreams, including the fear of the "what if." The fear of the "what if," is the fear of what if it happens. Having dreams and goals is quite different than accomplishing dreams and goals. Having them is exciting; accomplishing them, oddly enough, can be stressful and cause anxiety. Some people are afraid to go for their dreams and goals because they are unsure of whom they will be on the other side. Others fear fulfilling their dreams, thinking, *What then? After I reach my goals, what's left?*

Don't be discouraged by the fearful emotions you may experience about your dreams and goals. The amazing thing about going after what you genuinely desire is that another adventure is always waiting once the current goal is met.

A certain vulnerability comes into play when you truly decide to go after what you want. You are exposing your innermost desires to the world and hoping the world is kind. To create room for growth, you must take a chance and show the world a bit of vulnerability. The secret to this step is the more you show vulnerability, the easier it gets, and the more you will learn about whom you can show this side of yourself to. By taking this step, you will start to see change in your life, in your emotions, and in the way you approach sharing your thoughts, ideas, and goals.

You may feel you want to delay the positive change because you are not ready to take the leap, and that's okay. Just like when a light bulb starts to flicker and you think, *It can wait a little longer—I will live with the uncomfortable flicker for a while*, so also you have the choice to live with the uncomfortable flicker of delaying positive change. You may know the steps you should be taking to make positive change, but you may not be ready to take them. Identifying the needed change is important, and it is also important to feel you are ready to make the change.

The most difficult change is when someone forces it upon you before you are ready. You can live with the flicker for a while, and when you are ready, you will decide to change the light bulb. You may even wait until the light finally burns out to decide you are ready to make the change, but that step is up to you. It is yours to own, yours to act on, and yours to enjoy once completed. No one can force you to make positive changes. The choice must come from within. Once you find the strength, go for it—make the changes that make your life better!

CREATING GROWTH FOR YOURSELF

Wanting and desiring change is not enough. The third step is to follow through on habit-forming behavior and continuing to build the desire to do so. This is the action step. You will not change that light bulb until you are finally in the dark long enough, or you find the time to change the bulb. Change will not happen until you want it to happen, *and* you are willing to create the room and take action to create change.

You may find yourself living in the uncomfortable darkness of not changing the habits you know you need to until the darkness gets too difficult to live in. You may also find yourself living in the darkness because you don't know how to get out, and at some point, someone will come along to show you how to live in the light. You may remember someone doing this in the past. Sometimes you might not even realize you are living in the dark until someone shows you how to live in the light.

Creating room for growth starts with taking a good look at current habits that may be preventing you from reaching the success and happiness you dream about. After identifying those habits, the next step is identifying actions you can and need to take to create a healthier environment and make healthier choices. Finally, follow through. Good intentions without follow through will not create the positive change you desire. Follow through is where the magic of accomplishment lives.

CREATING GROWTH FOR OTHERS

Sometimes you grow, and sometimes you help others grow. When you find your light shining bright, it is time to help others who are in the dark. Everyone needs extra light at some point, and sharing your light with others makes it *and* their light grow stronger. You become stronger together. The amazing thing about light is that sharing it makes everyone's light brighter. The more light you share, the more light you have to share. It becomes a never-ending supply of strength and encouragement for all involved.

Sharing light can be as simple as sending a quick text to those around you who may be struggling. A simple act of kindness can brighten someone's day and lets them know they are cared for, even if from afar.

If you are feeling particularly strong right now, I encourage you to think of three people you interact with regularly who may be struggling in the dark. Send them each a text asking how they are doing and how you might encourage them in the following week. This simple exercise speaks to helping others strengthen their light, and in so doing, it also helps build and strengthen connections and your own light. When you are strong and have the energy, reach out to strengthen the relationships around you.

Sharing your light is the easiest way to build and strengthen connections. Sharing your light helps others feel cared for and connected to you. In that connection, they will want to reciprocate and share their light with you, thus making both of your lights brighter. This is a big part of the light bulb effect. When you support others, *both lights grow brighter*.

TROUBLESHOOTING

Sometimes, no matter how hard you try, you will be unable to find the motivation to choose the things you know are good for your life.

Here are some things you can try:

1. Recognize that intentionally ignoring a burned-out light bulb because another is providing light is okay. You are choosing to prioritize your time and focusing on more important things. In these circumstances, give yourself grace and compassion,

knowing and understanding that when the time is right, you will change what needs to be changed. Knowing what you need to do is not enough to accomplish it. Circumstances may keep you from making changes right now. If you know the change you should make but you are unable to make it now, give yourself grace. Make it when you can. Choose the positive choice when you can. Until then, don't just let it sit and stagnate. Think about it. Plan the change for when time allows so you are ready—but give yourself grace.

2. Sometimes you may choose to neglect a burned-out light bulb and decide to be in the darkness until you are ready to take on changing the light bulb so you can return to the light. Life can be overwhelming, and sometimes you won't have the energy to make the changes you know would benefit you. The act of delaying changing the light bulb may be the only thing you have energy to do presently.
3. Do your best to "hold space" for yourself and for others. To hold space means you are offering grace, room for growth, mistakes, and acceptance of where you are in your journey and where others are in theirs. Accept yourself and others as they are, that acceptance will help you and them grow. Set goals. Don't allow yourself to sit in this stage for too long or you will run the risk of becoming stagnant. On the opposite side of that, everyone has times when they just need to rest. If that is the stage you are in, take that time to rest. Don't get stuck in the mud and call it rest. Rest when rest is needed, but make progress where you can make progress.

SUMMARY

Creating room for growth starts from within. You can pull light from others while giving them light. Know that you are stronger when you share your light. Other people are stronger when you share your light. The more light you share, the more you will have to share. Be graceful and compassionate with yourself about the things you know you should do but are not ready or able do right now. When the time is right, you will progress. If the opportunity arises to make those healthy choices, don't delay. Make them when you can. If you are unable to make a healthy choice, be graceful to yourself until you are ready.

Don't get stuck in the mud. Give yourself grace to rest when rest is needed. Think about creating room for change and growth because in your thoughts you may uncover hidden motivation. As always, believe in yourself and the journey you are on. Though you will experience failure, that says nothing about the success you can achieve. The only thing that will hinder your success is if you decide to quit. Deciding not to move forward is deciding to quit. Stop and rest for a bit, but do not let yourself stay in that stage. Life wants you to accomplish more. Make room for rest and know that rest is moving you toward growth.

Chapter 8

SEEKING THE LIGHT

"Tomorrow may be fair, however stormy the sky of today."

— Lewis Howard Latimer,
Draftsperson for Thomas Edison in 1884

Whatever you may be going through, it can be difficult to see the light at the end. The most difficult parts of life can seem the darkest. One of the biggest concepts that helps me get through life's difficulties is to remember everything changes. This concept not only helps me get through the grim times, but it helps me appreciate the good times. That is because in the good times, I realize they will not last forever. I try to soak in every moment. On the other side of that thinking is the belief during tough times that they will not last forever either.

If the sky is stormy today, trust that the light may shine tomorrow. Everything changes. You may need to proactively seek the light, but also have faith in knowing it will come into your life. If you are in the darkness right now, know the darkness will pass. The darkness may try to make you believe it is permanent, but that is not true. Light will come if you keep trying. Keep seeking the light; you will find it.

THE DIM LIGHT BULB

Everyone experiences times when their light bulb is dim. In those times, it can be easy to believe you may never find the light you once carried. You may feel alone and isolated. The darkness may even be trying to make you believe no one could relate to your current circumstance. The darkness has a lot of power over thoughts, emotions, and actions. The more power it takes, the dimmer your light becomes. In these times, you must take action. Everything in your body and mind might be fighting against taking the needed action, but it can create the light you need. When the darkness is trying to grow within you, it is time to reach out for support.

Seeking strength from others' light when the darkness has become your closest friend conflicts with what the darkness wants you to do. Searching for and finding what may be the last bit of light within and using it to reach out to others can save your life. Reaching out to the trustworthy people around you is one of the greatest and most difficult actions when you get stuck in the darkness, but so much power resides in taking that action.

The darkness will try to dim your light in many ways, from overhearing people gossip about you to being mistreated by people you trust. The goal of darkness is to block as much light as possible from your life. Do not fear—there is hope in the darkness. Reaching out for support and seeking others' light provides strength. Sometimes you give the light to others, and sometimes you receive the light. To be balanced, both are needed as you interact with the world. No one is untouched by darkness, and everyone can use extra light.

Having a dim light bulb is not uncommon, but the darkness would like you to think it is. Remember, darkness tries to take away your power. It tries to make you believe you are less than you are. Darkness pushes the idea that you are not good enough. What's interesting is that everyone at some point struggles with these thoughts. The lies darkness tells are not creative or original. Many people struggle with the same dark thoughts. When you seek out others, this truth is brought to the light, and your power to fight darkness will start to increase.

In connection, light grows. When you reach out to others for support, your light will grow. Not everyone knows or understands what to do when someone reaches out for help. If you find yourself reaching out, but not getting the help you want, do *not* stop there. Try again. That is part of *The Light Bulb Effect*. Do *not* give up if you are not getting the results you desire. In that crucial moment, you need to try again. The magic of *The Light Bulb Effect* is in the follow-up. The magic is in trying again.

SEEKING THE LIGHT

As a single mom, I cannot tell you how many times I felt caught in the darkness. Occasionally, someone would appear at just the right moment to share some of their light with me. I experienced one of these times was when I was running errands and found myself at The Home Depot. On my way out, I ran into one of my favorite college professors. This was shortly after my divorce so not many people knew I was single. We caught up for a moment, and I told him about the divorce. He was kind, offering a genuinely attentive ear and some compassionate words. The entire interaction took less than ten minutes, but even six years later, I remember him sharing some of his light with me while I was stuck in the darkness. Events like this supply ongoing light. I can still reach back when I am struggling and remember this interaction and feel better. Had I not chosen to open up in that moment, he would not have known I was getting caught in the dark. Seeking the light from others may require genuine vulnerability.

When opportunity presents itself to offer genuine vulnerability to someone you know will protect and honor it, do it. In looking for light, your light will grow brighter, and that often requires you to invest genuine vulnerability.

Note that not everyone you cross paths with will honor your vulnerability, so be careful whom you share it with. Vulnerability is something to be earned through experiences and trust. You decide whom to open up to. As you continue your journey of vulnerability, it will get easier to tell your story and to identify whom you can and can't trust.

Your stories from the darkness really are not for everyone, but they should be shared with some. Nothing belongs in totality in the dark. Think of this as an internal challenge. Think of the people in your life who have earned the right to carry some of your darkness. A couple of people probably come to mind right away. Share your darkness with them so they can share their light with you. An amazing thing happens when you share darkness. Instead of darkness growing onto the other person, the light that is present grows for both people.

When you share darkness, you are not only sharing your struggle and seeking light, but you are giving the other person a huge compliment, telling them you trust them enough to let them see your darkness.

I have two extremely close friends who know everything about me. Our trust did not happen overnight. It took several years of working together, interacting, and taking steps to build our friendship in times of light and darkness. One time, we decided to go on a trip to Mexico together. A couple of days into the trip, we were lounging on the beach at the hotel when a pivotal moment happened.

On that beach in Mexico, we took a chance with each other and shared some very real, very genuine, and very vulnerable details about our lives. After the trip, we noticed the change in our relationship. Trust grew between the three of us, and so did the support. What we shared was special, it could be trusted, and we would support each other. That continues to this day. These two people know all my darkness and offer love and support anyway. Trust is there, so we know we can continue to share the darkness, and because of that, we are stronger together. My light is and will always be brighter because I have these two people in my life.

Having others you can share your darkness with is immensely important. Sharing your darkness with a trusted few is extremely important to growing your light. Sharing both your light and darkness with those you trust brings more light to the world and makes it a better place. The world is better when people learn to trust and share their light.

EXERCISE

Take a moment right now and list two people you trust with your darkness. If it is difficult to think of two people you trust implicitly, instead note the names of two people you want to grow to trust and work on sharing your darkness with. This is an important piece of growing your light. Though you might be tempted to skip this short activity, do not succumb to that temptation.

Begin to invest in the people you listed. Support them in their times of darkness and connect with them in your times of light. Growing your light takes positive action. Grow your light and the light of the people you listed before the darkness comes so when it does, you already have some resiliency built. Investing in these individuals can be as easy as sending them a text to say you are thinking about them. It could be scheduling a night out or a quick lunch. In building the connection, you will build and strengthen each other's light.

FINDING THE LIGHT

Light can be found outside of your friends and relatives. For some, their support system is not enough, and they may have had difficulty finding light within their friend or family groups. Not to worry because there are other ways to look for light and get help carrying your darkness. Finding light in this area still involves being brave and opening up with genuine vulnerability.

That takes me back to a quote from the movie *Bounce*, released in 2000, starring Ben Affleck and Gwyneth Paltrow. In one scene, Paltrow's character turns to Affleck's and says, "It's not brave if you're not scared." That quote has stuck with me for years and applies in this situation. It takes some courage to show others your darkness, and it is not brave if you're not scared. Sharing your darkness is not easy. It can be risky, but the reward is genuine connection. In connection there is light, and that light is how you fight off the darkness.

One way to find light outside of your immediate group is through counseling. You can find counselors in your local area at *PsychologyToday.com*. The website lets you search by area of expertise and location. It is a great tool for finding a provider who fits your desired criteria. Providers on this website include those who supply both telehealth and in-person services, so you can receive care from the comfort of your own home if that is something you are interested in.

You can also find light outside your immediate group through a mentor, coach, or advocate. These are all very individual options. A quick Google search and read of the individual's reviews can tell you a lot about the services and care they provide. Volunteer work, community classes, and getting involved in local activities are also good options for warding off the darkness and finding connection. Websites and social media sites like Facebook may help your search since they typically post events you can browse to see what you might like to get involved with.

SUMMARY

Fighting off the darkness is easier when you are looking for and investing in the light. Sometimes you need inspiration, and sometimes you give inspiration. By developing and investing in the connections around you, not only will you fight off the darkness and grow your own light, but you will start to make real, genuine connections with people you trust. As your light grows based on the people you choose to have in your life, you will also help grow their light. Darkness will always be there waiting, but its strength is diminished by the connections you build around yourself. The darkness becomes small in the light, and the light is strengthened by sharing your darkness with those who have earned that sacred trust. Be brave and choose to fight off the darkness with the strength of your vulnerability. Be scared and do it anyway.

Section 3

RECOGNIZING THE PEACE OF THE LIGHT BULB

"Stop thinking you need a miracle. Realize that you are a miracle."

— Mel Robins,
December 11, 2017, Twitter

Chapter 9

THE HURT LIGHT BULB

"Go as far as you can see; when you get there, you'll be able to see farther."

— J. P. Morgan,
American Financier

Though the beauty of a whole light bulb allows light to shine bright and strong, the hurt light bulb carries with it a mature kind of beauty. Even though a new light bulb begins its journey whole and, over time, gets scratches and scars, there is beauty in the pieces of the hurt bulb. When a bulb gets hurt, when it breaks, the pieces do not all break the same. The glass breaks at various places and creates both large pieces of glass and small shards. The way people break is similar. People experience diverse kinds of hurt, and they experience these hurts in their own unique ways. For example, the unique way one person hurts when they experience an affair is quite different from another person's experience of that same event. It's important to understand that everyone experiences events differently.

You have already experienced hurt in many ways, so your metaphorical light bulb may have scratches, scars, and some broken pieces of glass, but know that there is so much beauty in your piece and there is so much hope left to be uncovered. Everyone breaks at some point, whether by their own doing or by someone else's bad decisions. No one is untouched by hurt. The important question around these injuries is: What will you do with your broken pieces? No one gets to decide the answer to this question except you.

You can probably think of people who have shown amazing healing after experiencing a scratch or scar to their light bulb; they come out on the other side appearing even more brilliant. These people are called Light Healers. Not only have they learned how to heal themselves, but typically, they also know how to provide compassion, empathy, and grace to others; at times, they can offer paths of healing to aid others in their journey to healing. When their bulb cracked, they allowed the cracks to let the light in. It's in the cracks and brokenness that the light can come back in.

The opposite of Light Healers are Light Suckers. These people have walked away from hurt and injuries with a big chip in the glass of their bulb and have not allowed the light to fill the gap. People who carry a chip may even carry that chip as a badge of honor and use it as an excuse to hurt others. These people are called Light Suckers.

Light Healers have come upon patterns in life that have resulted in them being able to heal their cracks, chips, and scars. Light Suckers use their cracks, chips, and scars as an excuse to avoid the healing process; this results in them continuing to carry around their injuries rather than finding healing or comfort. Light Suckers deserve some understanding; as discussed in the last chapter, healing takes courage. If a Light Sucker has not yet found their source of support to draw courage from, it is more difficult for them to find their own inner healing. The understanding of why they hurt others does not excuse them from the consequences of hurting others.

WHEN HURT OCCURS

There are diverse kinds of hurts people can experience. Two highlighted here are Intentional Hurt and Unintentional Hurt. The ways Light Healers and Light Suckers respond to these two distinct kinds of hurt are vastly different. Though each hurt carries with it a different motive, pain is still caused to the recipient. This is an important element to observe because with each kind of hurt, some form of reconciliation is needed for healing to have room to occur.

Hurt is hurt to the person who experienced it. The way a person is hurt is not to be defined by the person who caused the hurt. The only one who can define the hurt is the person who received it—the recipient of the actions that caused the hurt. This is a very delicate topic to address because hurt can cause an array of emotions on both sides, ranging from confusion and anger to sadness and anxiety. Unresolved hurt remaining in any relationship can lead to serious emotional injuries that result in substantial amounts of mistrust and loss of connection.

Making room for healing is the responsibility of the person who caused the hurt as long as the person who received the injury is open to that action. If that sentence was difficult to read, give yourself some grace. If you have caused someone hurt, you may be carrying around hurt over that same situation yourself. It might be time to try to take some action if you have not done so already to heal the hurt on both sides. If you were the recipient of hurt and the person who was the cause of that hurt did not try to provide space for healing, you are not alone. These kinds of wounds can leave deep holes. Opportunities do not always exist for healing to occur how you would like. As unfortunate as that truth is, in those situations, self-healing can be sought after and achieved.

INTENTIONAL HURT

Intentional hurt is when someone causes pain to another, knowing their actions would not help that person. The example listed above, an affair, would fall under intentional hurt. When two people make a commitment and agree to trust each other, if one of them breaks that trust, they cause intentional hurt. Other actions that fall under intentional hurt include the basic three: lying, cheating, and stealing. As does any kind of mistreatment, such as physical, emotional, sexual, and financial abuse—which will all be addressed later in this book. Overall, intentional hurt occurs when someone makes a deliberate choice and knows another will experience a negative consequence because of that choice.

The Light Healer's response to causing intentional hurt varies drastically from that of the Light Sucker. When the Healers make an unwise decision that hurts someone they love, even though they made the decision, they often carry guilt. When Light Suckers make an unwise decision that hurts someone they love, they often blame someone or something else to deflect the responsibility and avoid confronting the hurt they caused.

Responses from both groups tend to be similar. When someone's intentional actions hurt another, the person being hurt is damaged emotionally and the relationship becomes distant until the injury is addressed. The best way to address an intentional injury caused is with humility, love, and patience. Saying that is easy; practicing it is a bit more difficult. It may mean giving the hurt person space to express their thoughts, feelings, and emotions about what was done.

Providing the hurt person an active listening ear is key. To set the tone for providing this kind of space, the first rule is *don't* interrupt the hurt person as they share their experience. The second rule is *don't* blame the hurt person for actions that caused the hurt. Finally, do not deflect responsibility—take ownership of your actions.

Anyone can easily think of a time when they were hurt and a time when they caused hurt. Remembering such times helps build empathy and understanding. You probably thought of someone who hurt you who did not go through the steps above. Maybe they did not give you space to share your thoughts and feelings about what their actions meant to you. If one does not give this space, it adds an unfortunate event on top of the hurtful event. It becomes a double injury. Not only did someone hurt you, but they hurt you again by not respecting you as you tried to heal.

Sometimes healing can't or won't come from the person who hurt you, but you can still achieve healing from within. You can discuss the situation with a trusted friend, family member, professional counselor, or mentor, or you might read a self-help book to get yourself to an introspective place. You do not need the person whose actions hurt you to validate your hurt. You know how they hurt you, that they hurt you, and the effect the hurt has had in your life. In a perfect world, they would give you space and care enough to walk with you through your healing. Unfortunately, that doesn't always happen. That is when it is important to reach within and find ways to heal yourself of the hurt you carry.

EXERCISE

Put this book down. Set a timer for five minutes. Reflect on a time you were hurt and how you can work to heal yourself. Journal your thoughts.

UNINTENTIONAL HURT

Unintentional hurt is when someone's actions hurt another without the doer of the action truly understanding the consequences. One particularly important and sometimes confusing thing to understand about unintentional hurt is that unintentional hurt is still hurtful. Our actions still hurt another, and the hurt still needs to be fixed. Just because the light bulb was damaged unintentionally does not mean it's fine and can be left as is. We still need to offer care and attention to rectify the damage we caused.

Usually, the responsibility for healing the situation falls on the party who caused the hurt, unless they do not know they caused an injury. If you have been hurt but the person who hurt you doesn't know it, then it's up to you to tell them. This provides space for reconciliation. If the hurt person doesn't speak up and the person who caused the hurt doesn't know they caused pain, distance can start to develop. This is dangerous in any kind of relationship because the hurt festers and grows.

Not telling the person who hurt you also robs them of the opportunity to rectify the situation. The exception is when it is unsafe to tell the person they hurt you. In that case, get the appropriate people or agencies involved to help rectify the situation. By acting on hurt and mending emotional injuries, you create space for healing. If no action is taken, the hurt lingers. When several instances of lingering hurt build up, the relationship will have a different, negative energy and can change for the worse.

Going back to when I broke the green light bulb, if I had missed some shards even after I vacuumed, and my kids had cut their feet, they would still be hurt. Even though I would not have tried to hurt them, I would have still caused the hurt done to them. Actions, even unintentional, can still cause pain, so it is important to acknowledge what you did. If I argue with my kids, saying I did not *mean* for them to cut their feet, it would not stop the bleeding. I still need to take care of their injuries and tend to them to help them heal. Even without the intent to hurt, they still cut their foot on the glass. Even though I thought I had picked up all the glass, the leftover pieces still caused damage, and because of that, I need to take care of the hurt even after I thought I already had done all I needed to do to correct the situation.

RECONCILIATION

Sometimes the responsibility for bringing attention to the damage falls on the person who caused the hurt, and sometimes it falls on the person who was hurt. Reconciliation is difficult. It feels vulnerable. It feels like taking a chance on something you are not sure will work out. With all that known emotional risk, it is still worth trying to heal.

Without working toward healing, relationships can stagnate, and that environment builds grudges. Grudges are like cancer for any relationship. They can start small and eat away at everything healthy that was once valued and loved, destroying the relationship. Therefore, facing difficulties head on with empathy and compassion is vital to the health and survival of every relationship. Reconciliation must be a core value held in high esteem and sought after when hurt is identified.

If you experience difficulty in and around reconciliation, you are not alone. You might have a tough time bringing attention to the hurt you experienced when the other person does not realize their actions hurt you. On the other hand, you might experience some difficulties acknowledging and accepting that you hurt someone. Both experiences may make you feel vulnerable when taking action to heal the hurt. It might seem easier just to let it go and not really deal with it—but be careful when you choose that path because it can be a cancer in your relationship that leaves space for grudges to grow.

How do you start the process of reconciliation? To offer some encouragement, know that anticipating a reconciliation conversation is worse than the act of reconciliation itself. Once you go through the steps, it becomes easier and easier.

First, start by admitting the hurt to yourself and acknowledging that it needs healing attention. This step is vital for both your heart and the other person's. This helps you avoid blame and remain focused on fixing the problem.

Second, reach out to the other person. Yes—this might cause you some anxiety, but that anxiety is a good sign. It means you are acting on something important to you. Ask the other person to go out for coffee, drinks, lunch, whatever. Tell them there is nothing to worry about, but you want to touch base with them. Telling them this ahead of time is comforting and tells them you are not there to argue.

Third, be open, compassionate, and empathetic. Share what you want to share, and then give them the floor! It is *very* important not to interrupt when they are sharing their perspective. After they are done sharing their thoughts, wait about ten seconds to make sure they are not going to add anything, and then you can respond. It is highly possible they will interrupt you, but do not interrupt them. Get into this habit.

Fourth, once you have acknowledged the hurt in your heart, invited them to a meeting, shared your thoughts, and listened to theirs—do *not* jump into your response. Instead, repeat what you heard them say. It could sound something like, "I heard you say you felt…when I did…. Did I get that right?" Make sure to say all three parts, and end with that question—"Did I get that right?" If they add more, then repeat those three steps again, until they tell you that you got what they said correctly. Going through this simple practice will help the other person feel heard and validated. Hopefully, they will reciprocate and listen patiently to what you have to say, but be warned, that is not always the case.

Reconciling is the primary goal. If that is not possible, take heart in knowing you gave it your best effort. You know you have not left anything unsaid.

We cannot control other people's responses, no matter how much we would like to. In a perfect world, reconciliation would always happen, but if you can't get that, you will know you tried your absolute best.

SELF-HEALING

Sometimes no matter what you do, you just will not find reconciliation.

That is when you must figure out how to work through the unresolved hurt without the other person. Whether you hurt someone or someone hurt you, there will be pain on both sides. Unresolved hurt can be extremely difficult to live with because it leaves behind unresolved feelings and a lack of closure. The situation has no end. This kind of wound continues to feel open and unhealed unless you take action to work through the pain for yourself.

You can work through the pain in many ways—some are listed below. The most important thing to consider if you are living with unresolved hurt is that it is up to you to find healing. Is this unfair? Absolutely! Do you still need to act to resolve the hurt you carry? Absolutely. If you do not act to resolve the hurt, you risk bleeding that hurt onto undeserving people. You do not want to hinder your future relationships because you still carry past hurt.

Here is where *The Light Bulb Effect* really comes into play. Realize everyone is broken, but there is so much beauty in the pieces. You are hurt and broken, and so is the other person. Hopefully, you will be able to reconcile, but if you can't, you need to focus on the beauty of your broken pieces and healing. The broken pieces are valuable, and if you only focus on your brokenness, the beauty in your pieces will pass you by. The beauty in your pieces reflects the beauty life has to offer. Keep working on seeing the beauty in your pieces instead of focusing on the pain. You are more worthy than you think, and through your journey of self-healing, you will continue to discover the ways your value plays out to create the healing you desire.

EXERCISE

Many self-care techniques exist, and you can focus on them to create an environment of healing for yourself when you are unable to reconcile with the other person. Review the following list and challenge yourself to try at least one of the suggestions. To prepare for these activities, think about a situation that created unresolved hurt.

1. Write a letter to your hurt self, from your healed self. Let your healed self guide your hurt self to healing through use of empathetic, encouraging, and hopeful words. Read this letter any time you feel the pain of the hurt.

2. This exercise takes a bit of planning, but this is a great releasing exercise. You will need a package of birthday candles, a plate, some twine, and matches. Sit down privately with your supplies and take out one candle for every person involved in the situation that caused you pain. Using your twine, tie the tip of the candlewicks together. Choose who or what each candle represents. It could be the people you would like to break ties with. Using a lit match, heat up the wax on the bottom of the candle and place all the candles on a plate so they are standing upright. Now, light the wicks of the candles that are tied together. Slowly release that person from your life as you watch the flame cut the metaphorical tie.

3. Sometimes processing and releasing the hurt occurs with other relationships, such as a counselor, mentor, or best friend. If the options above were not for you, think of someone you could call to schedule time to talk through your pain. A lot of healing comes with just telling your story and feeling heard.

4. Finally, write a letter to the person involved in the pain. You will not give the letter to the person, so write out everything you wish you could say to them. When you feel you got everything out, destroy the letter by (safely) lighting it on fire, shredding it, or ripping it into tiny pieces. However, you want to destroy it (safely), do that. Let this be a releasing ceremony for you where you purge the hurt and let go so you can find healing within.

SUMMARY

When you heal the hurt you carry, the broken pieces you carry from your light bulb grow stronger. Like the quote above says, when you go as far as you can, you will find yourself able to go even farther than you thought you could. The healing process makes your pieces stronger. You become stronger. You will continue to find strength you did not realize you had. This is where the beauty of healing is found. Forgiveness does not mean forgetting. It also doesn't mean going back to earlier boundaries. It means you remove the power this unfortunate situation held over you. You are letting it go.

Chapter 10

FINDING PEACE IN THE PIECES

"The task you are called upon to do may be difficult, as all great tasks are, but God's grace and strength are equal to the difficulty. You will succeed if you lay hold on them."

— Stephen J. Herben, *The Epworth Herald*, Chicago, Illinois, July 7, 1906
(Stephen J. Herben conducted Thomas Edison's burial service)

Putting the pieces back together and realizing they can be fixed is a solid reality for anyone willing to invest in the effort, but it does take both emotional work, and often, physical action. Finding peace among the pieces is not for the weak at heart. If you are willing to go after the peace you deserve, there is peace to be found. Difficult journeys can lead to beautiful outcomes.

The secret hidden in *The Light Bulb Effect* is that everyone has experienced brokenness. You may not realize it from the outside, but everyone who has ever lived has experienced some form of brokenness. The difference in each individual's outcome is how they dealt with their broken pieces.

What choices did they make? Did they choose to take steps to heal, or did they get caught up in the shards?

Since you are reading this book, it is probably accurate to think you are taking action to heal your broken parts. Taking action is such a crucial step in healing—way to go! As you continue to go through these chapters, you will continue your own personal healing journey. Having broken pieces shows you have participated in life's great journey. You are not alone in your brokenness, and you have so many amazing things to enjoy now and in the future. Do not lose hope.

DISCOVERING PEACE

At this point in your journey, you have probably tried to fix some of the broken pieces in your attempt to discover peace. Ask yourself if there are some broken pieces you have not yet been ready to look at. Not every peace you carry will be easy to process. Some will take a lot of emotional investment. Reflect on the broken pieces you have processed and healed up to this point. How did you feel during that journey? How did you feel after? As I've said, not all broken pieces can be healed with the other person, but self-healing can happen.

For the pieces you have not yet been able to heal, give yourself grace, but don't get caught in the time trap. The time trap is the "little white lie" we sometimes tell ourselves about how "there is always more time." You may be thinking, *There will be time for healing later*. That message could be doing more harm than good. By holding that belief, you are hanging on to hurt that could be getting in the way of your current joy and happiness.

Continue to discover your peace by taking a good look inside and asking yourself if you are carrying shards you really do need to let go of. You can identify which situations you need to let go of by asking yourself if they are producing healthy habits, joy, and happiness or stress, worry, or concern for your safety. Taking hold of your peace means making changes that can feel very painful in the moment. Choosing a little pain in the moment to create a better life for yourself and for the people around you will be worth the sacrifice. Granted, sometimes making changes now to create a better life involves more than a little pain. But the goal is joy and happiness. The pain that keeps you away from making the healthy choice is doing just that—keeping you away from making the healthy choice. Do not let the pain lie to you and make you believe brokenness is all you deserve.

SAYING GOODBYE

If you have not done so already, you will start to realize there are going to be pieces of your light bulb that no matter how hard you try, you just cannot fix. In those times, to find your peace, you will have to say goodbye to some things you have been holding onto. These things may include allowing people to treat you in a way you do not appreciate. Maybe you need to end a relationship or say goodbye to a friend. Whatever continues to cause pain will continue to break pieces of your light bulb. Of course, some things that cause you pain, unfortunately, will be beyond your control—these are not the things being addressed in this chapter. Such things beyond your control may include health uncertainty, watching your child make choices you anticipate will not create joy in their life, or political unrest. Saying goodbye to the things you know are unhealthy is really the focus of this section.

To begin, make sure you have a good support system around you. If you do not have this, start to build it. If you are unsure of how to start building your support system, begin by reaching out to those around you to let them know you are struggling. If you do not have that, then begin by getting involved in your community and setting a goal to make new connections. Saying goodbye starts with saying hello to others, and it is vastly important that you either have a support team around you or you begin to build one. Wherever you are in this area, it is never too late to start making and deepening connections.

Next, saying goodbye also involves setting boundaries. Where do you feel mistreated, overworked, or underappreciated? Think about boundaries you can set in these situations to create a healthier environment in which you can thrive. This may mean doing a bit of self-advocacy. It also means opening up to others about how you want to be treated.

A quick word of caution—if you desire to have conversations, do so with empathy. If you approach a boundary setting conversation out of anger and haste, it probably won't go well. Patience in boundary setting conversations goes a long way in making mutually beneficial progress. You are educating the recipient about yourself and how you like to be treated. That person is learning while you are advocating for your needs. Overall, some things just can't be fixed. In those moments, you will have to choose to say goodbye without resolving the situation with the other person(s).

FAILURE AND SUCCESS

Failed attempts at fixing your light bulb can lead to success. Failure is not the end; it's just a chance to learn another way something will not work.

In failure, it is important to self-reflect so you know what doesn't work and can avoid that approach in the future. You learn new approaches by reflecting on your failures. Attempting something, failing, and learning from the attempt lets you check that method off your list, instead of trying the same thing over and over. This truly takes a lot of personal investment through self-reflection about failure. It can be difficult to identify what led to failure, but if you think deeply and ask for outside input when helpful, you will be able to identify why a given approach failed and then move toward other approaches.

Just like Thomas Edison learned from each time he "failed" to invent the filament in his light bulb, you too will learn from your failures and grow. Each time you grow, you learn more about how failure can lead to success, and you get closer to finding inner peace. Failure and success are so closely related that they should be family. You really cannot have success without failure.

How do you feel when you fail? Do you give yourself space to try to fix the situation? Do you give yourself grace and forgiveness? Or do you sweep the failure under the rug? Sometimes *you* will be the person *you* need to forgive. You will be the one to whom you need to offer grace. Until you do this, you may not find the valuable success hidden in your failure—you may not find peace. Sometimes it is hardest to offer yourself grace and forgiveness—but this is such a vital part of discovering the relationship between failure, success, and finding your peace among your pieces.

Failed attempts to fix the bulb can lead to success—failure doesn't mean failure as long as you learn from it. Try again—try something different until you find success. You can move on to try other things that may be more successful because you have already learned ways that will not work.

REACHING OUT

As with everything that gets damaged, sometimes it is important to call in the experts. In searching for peace, you try your best to fix what you can, and then, if you are unable to fully complete the repair, you call in an expert. Just the other day, my dishwasher broke. We would load our dishes, push start, and listen to it run. But in the end, our dishes were still dirty. So, what did I do? I tore the dishwasher apart and consulted Google. With the dishwasher completely torn open and having done twenty minutes of research on Google, I felt like the expert. I identified the problem as one of the two motherboards not working properly. I thought, *I think I can fix this on my own!* So, I continued. I spent about an hour on hold with Maytag trying to find someone who could tell me which motherboard needed to be replaced—for whatever reason, the question was unanswerable. I then consulted my good friend Google again, looking at the price of both motherboards. They were between $200-$500. I had a fifty-fifty chance of choosing the correct replacement part. I decided to call a local repair shop to ask for advice. After talking with them for about fifteen minutes, they said they could fix it for about $200—and that included parts and labor—so I decided to have them fix the dishwasher.

Just like I did everything I could to fix the broken appliance, I am sure you have done the same in similar situations. Sometimes you take the initiative to heal yourself because you have the skills to mend the broken pieces. Sometimes it benefits you more to call in the experts. Trying your best to fix what you can and then calling in the experts to help is a super-strength! Knowing when to ask for help makes a dramatic difference in the healing process. Not asking for help when you need it can hinder your growth. Don't hesitate to ask for help when it is beneficial to do so.

Help can come in many forms. Counseling, mentoring, and holistic healing can make an enormous difference in the healing process. For some, working with a doctor to use medications to balance your body's chemistry is a vital step in healing your metaphorical light bulb. Reaching out to ask for guidance creates an amazing superpower of knowledge and experience you may not already have in your toolbelt. Being able to soak up insight from others along your path to healing allows you to speed up your own journey to finding peace.

SUMMARY

Do not be afraid to reach out for help, and do not think anything negative about yourself because you reached out for help. Instead, think of the act of reaching out for help as an asset. Being able to open up to another about your struggle allows them to help you through those struggles, making them lighter. When you lighten your load this way, you make more room for healing. If you have been hesitant to reach out for help with a current situation, let this be the little push you need. Let this be the sign you have been looking for. It is time to experience the healing you deserve. It is time to reach out to a friend, counselor, mentor, or doctor. You become your own hero, your own protector, when you advocate for the healthy things you need that lead to achieving your goals. The time is now. Choose to lighten your load so you can find the peace you have been looking for. You still have so much hope.

Hope and healing are yours. You've got this!

Chapter 11

HOLDING SPACE FOR HEALING

"I want to make this perfectly clear: you can be sure that I will never be a yes-man except to my own conscience."

— Charles Edison,
Son of Thomas Edison and Mina Miller Edison

Have you ever felt that you tried a million ways to heal, but no matter what you did, you didn't make the kind of progress you would like to achieve? Occasionally, the things you do to heal just do not work. In these situations, you may need to replace parts of your inner light bulb as opposed to trying to fix them. That may be the most effective solution to meeting your goals.

Replacing parts of your light bulb can be tense because it involves letting go of things that, no matter what you do, do not serve you well. In these critical times, it is important to learn how to hold space for self-healing and the transition involved in that process. If, and probably when, you find yourself in this situation, you will be surprised at how much your inner strength comes out and guides you. Though you may feel alone at times, know your strength will not leave you. When you feel weak and you choose to carry on, your strength is working full force to help guide you through the transition of healing.

SCRIPTS

Everyone carries scripts around with them. A script is any repeated message you have told yourself for a long time, whether positive or negative. Scripts are a lot like positive or negative self-talk. Scripts serve a powerful purpose unless you have adopted a negative script. Some scripts may be untrue, and some may be outdated. Outdated scripts are messages that served you well in the past but are hindering your growth now. A script might have helped you survive an unhealthy situation, but it might have expired and become a negative and unhealthy script to carry now and into your future.

EXERCISE

1. Think back at least five years. Write a list of at least five positive scripts you carry with you from that time. An example of a positive script could be something like, "I am a valuable person and add positivity to the world."

2. On the opposite side, think back over that same period for outdated scripts you continue to carry. List them. A negative script could be something like, "I am in survival mode and will do what I have to do." Think about releasing these negative scripts you still carry as you read through this chapter.

The outdated script above, "I am in survival mode and will do what I have to do," has a time and place to be true and carried close to your heart. But once you no longer need it to survive, continuing to carry an outdated script such as that could cause more damage. Such a script might lead you to make rushed decisions as you focus on surviving rather than thriving. Once you are beyond survival mode, let that script go so you can stop making decisions based only on survival and focus on thriving.

Both outdated and current scripts provide comfort, and if comfort were all you were seeking, keeping all your scripts would be a good thing. If you are looking to evolve along your journey, revisit the scripts you carry to ensure they are evolving with you. This is an important part of healing your broken pieces.

If you lived in a small house that was well lit with only five light bulbs and then moved into a house twice the size, you would have to rethink your lighting needs. You might leave the bulbs in the old house for the new owners. Even if you kept the bulbs, you would add more to ensure you had enough light to be comfortable in your new house. The scripts you carry are the same. As you develop and grow, you need new scripts, unless the old ones are healthy messages you tell yourself. Even in that situation, you want to add more scripts to match your personal growth.

Take a closer look at the scripts you journaled about above. You have your first list, which are statements of strength, and your second list, which are scripts you may need to let go of. Spend a couple of minutes journaling about the outdated scripts. Think about what makes them outdated, and what an updated script would look like.

COPING SKILLS

Like outdated scripts, you will also want to look at the coping skills you carry and replace the outdated ones. A coping skill is a method you use to help reduce negative emotional distress. Coping skills differ from scripts you carry in that the scripts are messages you have carried with you for several years. On the other side, a coping skill is an action you take to help alleviate the physical, mental, or emotional stress you are feeling in any situation. You might have coping skills, just like scripts, that you have carried for years. And just like the scripts you carry, you must occasionally evaluate your coping skills to ensure they are evolving as you evolve. Using outdated coping skills might lead to negative outcomes.

One example of coping skills can be seen in people who have experienced some form of trauma. In trauma, whether emotional, physical, or other, people develop coping skills to survive. If they continue to use the coping skills they developed to survive trauma in non-traumatic situations, the outcome could be negative. For instance, if you had a partner who cheated on you and you eventually broke off the relationship, you may find it difficult to trust a new partner. Mistrust is an outdated coping skill—it no longer serves you.

Being afraid to trust again is a normal reaction when approaching a new relationship, but it is also outdated. You do need time to heal and rebuild trust so you can carry it into the new relationship, and you will most likely get triggered when you don't know where your partner is, but over time, if you are in a healthy relationship, that old, outdated coping skill will go away. As your new partner builds your trust, the outdated coping skill should slowly dissipate.

EXERCISE

1. Just like you did above, write five healthy coping skills you currently use to deescalate emotional distress when you feel it coming on.
2. List a couple of outdated coping skills you still carry with you.
3. Finally, think about the outdated coping skills and write down their counterpart, the healthy skills you would like those unhealthy coping skills to evolve into.

By identifying the positive and outdated coping skills you carry, you can work to turn the outdated skills into strengths. Every weakness you carry is just a strength waiting to be balanced. Once you can balance a weakness, it can become a strength. Strengths are the same. If a strength gets out of balance, it can become a weakness. It is a strength because you have learned how to keep it in balance, in its sweet spot. This is another way to look at the coping skills you carry.

EMOTIONS

To hold space for healing, discussing emotions is important. Obviously, you have negative and positive emotions, but confusion can exist in how you look at emotions typically labeled negative. Positive emotions are easy to spot because they tell you when you are having an enjoyable time, maintaining a healthy lifestyle, and developing positive relationships. You know these things are "good" by the emotions your system sends you, such as love, joy, hope, and an overall feeling of happiness.

Emotions typically labeled negative can be a bit trickier. Your emotional system is set up to give you signals to help you survive and thrive. Some emotions, such as anxiety, have gotten a bad rap. Each emotion you feel is your system trying to send you a message. For example, when people feel anxious, they tend to label it as a negative emotion and try to get rid of the anxiety. I want to challenge this approach to anxiety and other "negative" emotions. Continuing with the example of anxiety, if you are anxious, instead of trying to make it go away, what if you tried to embrace it and asked what it was trying to tell you? Anxiety, though it feels negative, serves a purpose. It is trying to alert you that something is off. The anxiety might be trying to help you thrive by making you a bit uncomfortable so you are motivated to act.

Anxiety is an easy example because most adults have experienced some form of anxiety. But this can apply to other "negative" emotions as well. In fact, the emotions our society has labeled negative might not be negative at all. They are just labeled negative because they feel bad. But they are designed to motivate us to act to relieve discomfort. They are designed to get us moving to figure out what is going badly in any given situation so we can act and experience a healthy environment. When we feel uncomfortable, we find the motivation to act to change a situation for the better.

The next time you feel emotions you identify as negative, metaphorically ask the emotion, "What are you trying to tell me?" See if you get an answer, or maybe you'll gain insight and the motivation to act in some area your emotional system knows can be better.

Note that this discussion is about low to medium anxiety. It is not about the intense anxiety people may feel when their body, mind, and emotional systems are out of balance. In those situations, it is always best to seek outside help, such as counseling, medication, holistic approaches, and other forms of healing.

HOLDING SPACE FOR HEALING

In the end, you must answer to yourself. Creating space for healing benefits you and the people around you, but ultimately, it is about your own well-being. Healing your emotions and the energy around you is for your own conscience and overall health. Continue to create and hold space so you can evolve and develop. Continue to support yourself just as you would give space to your closest friend when they are struggling.

One amazing introspective activity you can do in a challenging time to create space for healing is to imagine the five-year-old you. Imagine you are protecting them, wanting to give them the best life possible. When you create space for your brokenness to heal, you heal that inner five-year-old you. You tell them they are protected, valued, and cherished, and that things will not always be painful. If the brokenness you carry did not start that early, you may imagine yourself a little older. Whatever age you choose, the goal is the same: to provide your inner child with the love, protection, comfort, and care you might not have received from the people you needed it from the most.

Holding space and getting to the place where you can do so in an open and engaging way can take some practice. You might feel silly. You might feel exposed. Whatever emotions come up for you as you continue this practice, remember negative emotions may not actually be negative. Those emotions, though uncomfortable, could be trying to communicate a golden nugget of truth. Sit with those emotions, and ask them what they are trying to tell you. Spend some time reflecting and do some journaling. So much healing is waiting for you as you continue this work. Good luck!

THE SEARCH CONTINUES

Now that you have learned about scripts, coping skills, and emotions, your search for healing will continue to evolve and deepen. Looking for and finding the kinds of solutions that *will* work for you will be an exciting and ongoing journey. Finding and choosing healthy scripts, coping skills, and emotions will deepen your growth and bring you to new levels of understanding. Not only will you continue maintaining and creating new, healthier habits, but you will observe healthy habits in others you may want to adopt.

Always be on the lookout for what makes those you admire successful. Search, observe, and figure out what they are doing to attain the things you would also like to have. Sometimes the best teacher is observation. As the saying goes, the best compliment is replication. Try the skill of replication on for yourself.

Searching for the things you want to implement is mostly a trial-and-error process. Something that works for someone else might not work for you. But it might! It goes back to the concept I've used throughout this book—do not be afraid to fail; be afraid not to try. Try the skills you see being used by those you admire. If a skill works for you, great. You just learned something new about yourself. If it does not, could a slight change make it work for you? Try that. If it does not work at all, you have learned a way that is not for you. You have identified another skill that is not helpful to your journey, and you don't need to spend any more time trying it. You can move on with confidence.

Doing your best means making educated guesses about what will work for you. When you guess and try something, each attempt teaches you more about your success, what works, what does not, and what might need to be modified. In the end, you answer to your own conscience regarding what fits your life best. If you are eighteen or older, you only have to answer to yourself. You don't have to do what others want you to do or think is best for you. Do what you find creates the most success in moving toward your goals. This creates the space for healing.

SUMMARY

Creating space for healing is an important and intentional act that will help you achieve the results you want. The process takes work, investment, and endurance. You have it in you to experience everything you desire if you are willing to stick with the process until you reach your goals. Of course, you will experience ups and downs, but know those are all part of the process. In the counseling world, professional counselors often say, "Trust the process." It may feel like a never-ending process, but if you continue to put in the work, the process will lead you to healthy results. Trusting the process of your healing journey includes trusting yourself and ensuring you don't stop when you fail—giving up is the only way the space for healing can be taken from you. Like anything important, healing takes time. Trusting the process takes time. You are worth both the investment in healing and the time it takes to work through the process. If that statement is difficult to swallow, if it is hard to believe, not to worry—we are going through this journey together. Keep reading.

Section 4

DEVELOPING THE LIGHT BULB OF LEADERSHIP

You didn't grow up driving a car…you figured it out.

— Gary Vaynerchuk,
American Serial Entrepreneur

Chapter 12

SHARING YOUR LIGHT

"The seeds of great discoveries are constantly floating around us, but they only take root in minds well prepared to receive them."

— Joseph Henry,
Built One of the First Electromagnetic Motors

Going through the steps up to this point has provided the opportunity to do a lot of self-reflection and work on your inner light bulb. Now it is time to take what you have learned, thought about, and practiced thus far in this book, out into the world. The light bulb of leadership is about dynamically leading yourself and others to success. If you only worked on yourself and did not share your light, the world would not be as bright. You have light within to share, and when the time is right to share it, you will know. Sharing your light can create a mix of emotions. Remember to embrace those emotions and ask what they are trying to tell you.

The serendipitous effect of leading while sharing your light is your light grows stronger as you invest in other people. As you lead others and teach them, you will find yourself on a learning journey. Leading and serving others is not completely altruistic because everyone benefits, even you.

That is how we are designed. We are designed to experience mutually beneficial results from acts that appear altruistic. Receiving good feelings is part of the reward of being a leader, and those good feelings lead to wanting to invest in others even more. The more you do it, the more you will want to do it!

SERVING OTHERS

The secret to leading is serving. I found this to be true through years of owning and managing a successful counseling agency in Idaho. When I first opened the agency, I had a lot to learn. Unfortunately, with leadership when you make mistakes, they are very public. Those you lead often witness some or all the mistakes you make; thus, it is of the utmost importance that leaders stay humble, transparent, and collaborative. My master's degree is in marriage and family counseling, so I had no training or experience operating a business—I really had no idea what I was doing. I made my best guesses, made some mistakes, had some successes, and along the way, figured out how to do it successfully.

Today, service is one of the most important qualities I continue to grow in myself as a leader and in those who become leaders within my agency. When I hire someone, I tend to have a conversation with them about our mindset. I tell them that when they are employed by Family Counseling Services, I work for them. I explain that means it is my responsibility to ensure they have the training, supplies, and support they need to do their job. I want them to know if they do not have those tools, to tell me so I can continue to serve them until they feel confident in those areas. I also encourage them to come to me if they find something that will make their job easier. The leader's job is to support their staff. Leaders do this by serving their people and ensuring they are equipped with the tools, education, and support they need to grow and be successful.

The agency has grown over the years, and now others do the hiring. Guess what I do for them? I mentor them. I make sure they have the tools, supplies, support, and education to train high-quality leaders who will integrate into and add to the culture of the agency.

No matter what position you hold, if you are a leader in any aspect of your life, know that leadership is more about serving than leading. Leadership is more about ensuring those you lead have what they need to grow and be successful. At its core, being a leader is being comfortable with being humble.

The next quality in ensuring you are a good leader is openly acting on mistakes you make in a collaborative way. Are you a leader? You will make mistakes. This is something you must get used to. If you are not a leader at work, you may be a leader at home with your kids. If you don't have kids, you may be seen as a leader among your friends or family. Wherever someone looks up to you, you are, at times, a leader to them, and getting comfortable with the idea that you will make mistakes will make your partnership even stronger.

How do you approach your mistakes? Start by ensuring you understand the mistake. You might start by asking the person or people involved whether they would be willing to share their thoughts. If you are in business, you may need to do a bit of research to understand the mistake's effects before moving on to the next stage.

Once you understand the mistake and how it affected those around you, becoming comfortable with being humble makes a dramatic difference in the situation. The next step is to admit to making the mistake and talking about what you are doing to rectify the situation. You will find yourself on the hot seat sometimes, having to answer some difficult questions. When you do make a mistake, be open to discussing it, and do your best not to defend yourself. Own the mistake, and show those involved you will diligently look for the best solution for rectifying the situation.

SERVING YOURSELF

In the areas where people see you as a leader, know you don't only serve them but yourself as well. What does that mean? It means not only ensuring your people have the tools, education, and support they need to be successful, but you do too. After a couple of years of running the counseling center, I decided to invest in educating myself about business. I signed up for a series of post-graduate classes through a local organization. Once a month, I was out of the office for an entire day learning about how to run a business.

Taking this action paid off twofold. First, it prepared me to be a better leader, ensuring I understood employment law, expectations, human resources dynamics, and so on. Second, it showed my staff I understood I needed to improve in some areas, so I was investing both time and money to ensure I was making the best decisions for everyone. I often tell my staff I take very seriously the fact that their grocery money comes directly from the decisions I make daily. They rely on me to make the best decisions possible, so I do everything I can to protect their paycheck and the agency alike so both can thrive.

It is vitally important for a leader to ensure they have the education, tools, and support needed to successfully lead. Reflect on those three areas, asking yourself the following questions:

1. Do I have the *tools* I need to be a successful leader?
2. Am I lacking the *knowledge* to accomplish the tasks others look to me to accomplish?
3. Do I have the *support* around me to feel confident in both making decisions and rectifying mistakes, and can I get through both of those processes successfully when they present themselves?

EXERCISE

Spend time journaling about the actions you can take to strengthen the areas listed above that are not yet where you would like them to be.

CHOOSING YOUR LEADER

Every leader needs a leader. You will never "arrive" and be done learning. Being the best leader you can be means always growing. The best way to do this is choosing someone you trust and respect who is successful in the areas you want to be successful in to mentor you. Yes, you can read a book, listen to a lecture, watch YouTube, and even TikTok, and get some great ideas and advice. Those approaches have some good things to offer, but having someone who can personally hold you accountable and continue to push you toward your goals will help you reach higher and achieve greater things than you could by just doing it on your own.

When choosing a mentor, make sure you are choosing someone you feel has achieved more than you have so far. You want them to teach you, inspire you, and stretch you. You can pick a friend, but my best advice is to choose a professional—a business coach, life coach, or someone you look up to who has achieved a higher level of success in the area in which you want to grow. Meet them monthly, at a minimum.

Discuss your fears, hopes, and failures with your mentor. Brainstorm solutions to the roadblocks you are experiencing that prevent you from reaching the things you want. When you discuss setting a goal, make sure they are just a bit bigger than what you feel comfortable with. Reach higher than you think you can because, if you do not, you will be selling yourself short. Do not let your doubts get in the way of reaching higher.

Mentoring of this kind is different from professional counseling in the sense that professional counseling focuses on resolving emotional distress and healing trauma. Mentoring and coaching are more about looking to the future, setting personal and professional goals, and having a cheerleader who also pushes you to reach even higher. Healing is not the primary purpose of choosing a mentor or coach, though some healing will occur. If you are looking for healing, find a counselor to focus on the healing elements of your journey and find someone else to be your mentor.

Choose your mentor wisely. Choosing a mentor can be a lot like dating. I tell my counseling clients sometimes you must meet a couple of different professionals to see which you think will be the best fit for you. It is okay if you choose a mentor who doesn't end up being a good fit. If that happens, have an open conversation and tell them you want to try a different approach. You are your best advocate when it comes to the kind of leader you want mentoring you, but the overall lesson is, if you are a leader, you need a leader as well. Everyone should have some kind of mentor. As you know by now, life is painful, so having a strong mentor can help guide you through some events and help you avoid others. We cannot do this alone; life is better when we have people in our corner looking out for us.

BEING CHOSEN

One of the best compliments you can receive is being chosen to be someone's mentor. When this happens, you will want to ensure you can be the best leader for them possible. You do this by not only investing in them, but in yourself as well. Sometimes people will choose you as their mentor, and sometimes people will get assigned to you—as is the case in a work environment. Either way, you will eventually find yourself in a mentor/leadership role at some point.

Dynamically leading yourself and others to success is a sacred process. You are serving each other, growing, and collaborating for the purpose of finding and achieving success. To go through an experience in which you know you played a key role in improving someone's life is an incredible event. What better experience to have than helping someone achieve a happier and healthier life?

This discussion reminds me of Helen Keller and Anne Sullivan. You probably know Helen Keller was unable to see or hear after a severe illness she contracted when she was only nineteen months old. Anne Sullivan was the teacher who helped inspire Keller to learn to communicate. I often talk about this story at my agency, especially with new staff. Leaders not only teach and inspire but also learn and get inspired in the process. Serving others, especially when they choose you, can be very rewarding.

And if the person did not choose you? Then it is of utmost importance to first build rapport. The person you lead may not care what you have to say until they understand you care about their well-being and success. You can't care about those things until you get to know the person and learn about their interests, goals, and passions. When you are leading someone who doesn't feel connected to you already, make sure *you* understand the value you bring to the relationship. Set aside time to intentionally and truly get to know them. Help them realize what they value is important to you.

A terrific book on this topic is *How to Win Friends and Influence People* by Dale Carnegie. This book takes an in-depth look at simple things you can do to create and strengthen relationships. As a leader, this book should be in your toolbelt.

SUMMARY

Leaders need their own leaders so they can be the best leader they can be to others. That's a tongue twister! To inspire others, you need to be able to find inspiration of your own. To help others grow, you need to keep searching and growing. Being the best leader you can be begins with your own journey. Don't be complacent. If you don't move forward and grow, you get stagnant, and you will not be as effective as you could be. Reach out for extra support. Make sure both you and your mentee have the tools, education, and support you need to meet the goals you have for yourselves. If you find you are lacking in one of those three areas, work on that area. Get help. Get educated. Finding that balance for yourself will help you create that balance in your mentee's life as well. I can think of no better job than being someone else's inspiration!

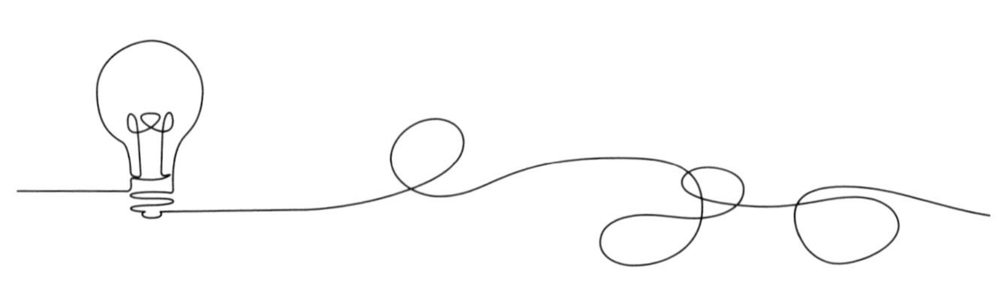

Chapter 13

TRANSFORMATIONAL CHANGE

"...a deeper interest in the moon than I ever felt before."

— Warren De La Rue,
Creator of One of the World's First Electric Light Bulbs

The light bulb of transformation is illuminated by strengthening the light within and around you. About five years ago, I decided to take my staff on a winter retreat. I had wanted to do this for years, so I planned out everything. I rented a cabin. The parking lot was about a mile away and we snowshoed into the cabin. I made two sleds we tied to our waists to haul some of the heavier items instead of carrying everything on our backs.

I knew this trip would challenge some, but I felt I had enough rapport with them to push them a bit beyond their comfort zones. The retreat was a group bonding exercise with some required annual training thrown in. The trip started off excellently. We snowshoed into the cabin, got settled, and ate dinner together. We also got through some training. Everything had come together as planned.

The next day, we made breakfast, did some more training, and got our snow gear on to go for a hike. I knew there was a hot spring nearby, and I wanted to take the group to find it. We were close to the main highway, so there was no substantial risk of getting lost as we searched for the spring. After about an hour of hiking, we had not found the spring. I asked the group if they wanted to continue. Half said yes, and the other half wanted to go back to the cabin, so we split up.

But those who remained were all in! So confidently, we carried on in search of the spring. The sure way to find the spring was to walk to the highway and follow it to the hot springs path, so we did that. Our reward was sitting in the snow with nature surrounding us while enjoying one of Idaho's treasured hot springs.

One supervisor on that trip, stayed at the agency for almost ten years! My experience with and her sense of adventure was so positive. As her boss, observing her approach to life taught me a lot about the kind of employee she was and would always be. She earned a promotion to clinical supervisor and served in that role for several years before going out on her own. Because she was willing to take a chance in that moment on the retreat, I saw how she would react to making tough decisions. Taking that one chance led to the change in her position at the agency. I could tell that her leadership style would show the staff she was confident, collaborative, and seeking to work for the team's greater good.

In the same way, this supervisor chose to take a chance and keep going on the retreat, so transforming your life begins with taking a chance. Change is not found in routine. Change happens when you take a chance, get out of your routine, and try something different. Sometimes it will work, and sometimes it will not work. Either way, you learn something new about yourself and those around you.

MOTIVATION AND DISCIPLINE

Change is easy when you are motivated. So many variables can lead someone to want to change and improve their situation. When the desire to change presents itself, act! That's when you feel like you are hitting the road running. You might feel like you already have ideas you want to try, and you are going for it.

At times, you may feel afraid to start a project. Maybe you feel the project will fail if you lose your motivation. In that moment, you are faced with a "fork in the road" kind of decision. When you can't find the motivation, you need to allow discipline to take over. Motivation is never going to be enough to fully accomplish a goal. If you are waiting for the motivation to strike before you to start or continue a project, and you are relying on that to get you through, it will not happen. Motivation is a short-term emotion. Discipline is needed to achieve your goals.

When motivation wanes, discipline must take over. Discipline is the secret to successful transformation. Discipline is a requirement and must be in place to create change. You strengthen discipline by making hard, healthy choices. Each time you make a difficult yet healthy choice, your discipline gets stronger. Making the hard choice in moments of temptation leads you to desired outcomes.

TAKING THE RISK

Change does not come without some risk. When you do something new, you don't know for sure it will go your way, but you try and hope it works out. If it does not, don't worry. Pick yourself up, dust yourself off, and try again.

I found success through risk when I started the counseling agency. I did this with an initial budget of only $700. When I signed the first lease, the rent was just over $700—and that was more than my mortgage at the time. Paying more rent for the office than my mortgage made me nervous. In the end, it went my way and the new agency blossomed. If you have a dream and you feel you can achieve it, start taking steps to work toward it now. You may not see how it is going to play out, but if you don't start, you will never know. If you never try, you will never grow. Do not be afraid of feelings. Do not be afraid of being nervous about taking a well-thought-out risk. Like the cliché says, be afraid of never trying. Every time you try and fail, you learn something new to help you get further on your next attempt.

CONFIDENCE

Confidence will always be a struggle for me. I know a lot of people can relate, but over the years, as I've tried and succeeded at different things, my confidence has grown. As I sit in my kitchen drafting this book, I know one of my strengths is believing in myself and that I can get the job done. Notice I didn't say I would get the job done perfectly. But I strongly believe if I have a job to do, I will figure out how to do it. I believe in myself and my ability to get things done when I try, no matter how many attempts it takes me. I understand I may fail along the way, and I accept that. One difficult thing I've experienced is that some failures as a business owner are very public, but I believe in myself and my ability to succeed, so I continue to push through the process, believing I will accomplish my goal.

As you read this book, you may be thinking about your strengths and weaknesses. You might be thinking about where you feel confident and where you feel a bit more reserved. Knowing these things about yourself will build your confidence and continue to lead you to the transformation you desire. No one arrives at confidence without some bumps, bruises, and scratches on their metaphorical light bulb. How you respond to those events, how you hang on, how you get through, becomes your superpower.

When you have a deep interest, it will drive you forward. Continue to have a deep interest in your growth, your transformation, and your evolution. That will be the driving force for the positive changes in your life, your job, and your relationships. All it takes for change to thrive is giving growth a chance. Let change show you what it is capable of. Give it some space to grow. Water it. Give it food as you would a plant, and see what happens.

Give it your best shot. Go after the goal you do not think you can accomplish. If you have seen someone accomplish what you want to do, if your goal is humanly possible, then go after it. The worst-case scenario is that it doesn't happen and you end up right where you are now—but the best-case scenario is success!

EXERCISE

1. If you could not fail, what three goals would you like to accomplish in the next twelve months?
2. Write out the first step to accomplishing the goals you listed.
3. Write the name of someone you can reach out to who will hold you accountable for going after at least one of the above goals.

ACCOUNTABILITY

Your challenge is to call the person you listed above and invite them into your journey. Ask them if they would hold you accountable by giving you a call to check in on your progress. If you accomplish the goal, move on to the next one. You will find you can do more amazing things than you thought possible.

Change needs accountability. Sure, you can go at it on your own, but when you have someone checking on you, you will make more progress than if you are working on your own. You will notice you can accomplish some tasks on your own without a push from someone outside the situation. If that is the case, go for it. But you will sometimes face tasks that, no matter how much you want them and how much you try, you just cannot get done. That is when reaching out to a friend, mentor, or coach helps most.

It is vital to understand that just because you can't reach a goal on your own does not mean you can't reach that goal. You need to think about ways to approach the goal. Inviting a third party into the process is a wonderful way to push yourself toward the things you want to accomplish. A mentor or coach can help you find strategies you may have never thought of on your own. Introducing new methods to get what you want can get you back on track. It can be where inspiration meets motivation.

Do not stop just because you hit a roadblock. Take time to think about what could remove the roadblock from your path. You can almost always find a way to achieve what you desire; you just have to spend some time thinking, brainstorming, and finding a path that will lead to your desired destination.

GENERAL VERSUS SPECIFIC GOALS

Note that some specific goals may never be attainable. An example of an unattainable goal would be marrying someone who is not interested in you as opposed to the general goal of marrying someone with whom you will be happy. Don't make your goal too specific or you may end up backing yourself into an unrealistic corner.

A specific goal is focusing on one very precise outcome, whereas a general goal is focusing on an outcome you can achieve through various paths. When thinking about change and the goals you want to implement, make sure your goals are general enough to allow several avenues to success, and not so specific that if one opportunity fails, you are left in the dark. Goals must carry hope to survive.

SUMMARY

Transformational change does not happen by accident. It takes intention, action, and the desire to experience this kind of shift. Sometimes, you will not be able to overcome the roadblocks in your path alone. When that happens, contacting a friend, mentor, or coach to help you is highly beneficial. Change takes work. You have it in you. Do not quit. Rest, but do not quit. Do not let yourself quit and call it resting. Keep your momentum even if you are just making an inch of progress every day. A little movement toward the change you desire is better than no movement at all. Be like Dory and keep swimming.

Chapter 14

THE LIGHT BULB OF EMPOWERMENT

"You must be ready to give up even the most attractive ideas when experiment shows them to be wrong."

— Alessandro Volta,
Inventor of the Electric Battery

Empowerment comes both from within and from the world around you. It is about the decisions you make daily. The boundaries you keep. The way you approach your work. The way you choose to maintain relationships. The light bulb of empowerment is about creating and maintaining sustainable change within your light to make you brighter and stronger.

To be empowered is to understand you have the strength to accomplish what is expected of you in a healthy way. One of the interesting things about empowerment is you will not feel empowered until you take action toward doing the thing you desire. The feeling of empowerment comes from knowing you can succeed, but you really cannot know how to succeed until you take the chance to find out. The more chances you take, the more empowered you will feel.

Here's a quick word of caution and reminder that when you take chances, you will often fail. And when you fail, it is important not to give up. Get back up, dust yourself off, and try again, because those repeated attempts are where success is found, where empowerment is experienced. Success is uncovered where failure is discovered.

EMPOWERMENT OF PROTECTION

When my daughter was younger, she joined a dance team. The experience began as an exciting adventure. Watching her learn, grow, and have fun was really rewarding. She was very excited to be accepted after tryouts and had a blast during her first year on the team. She put a lot of effort into attending practices, building relationships, and trying her best.

When the second year came around, she tried out and once again made the team. The same thing happened with the third year—but in the third year, something was different. She was often withdrawn when she came home from dance. We talked several times about whether she wanted to continue dance. She always said yes. One night at pickup, she came out of practice limping. She told me she thought she needed to go to the doctor to get her foot looked at. The doctor confirmed she had broken her foot and would need to see a specialist. I informed the coach that night about the injury that occurred in class.

Recovery was long! Since she was on the team, she continued to attend practices, but she did not participate. Several doctor visits came and went—the break was serious. Luckily, she didn't need surgery, just time to heal, which eventually happened. Things were hopefully going to get back to normal…but that is when I learned she was being bullied. She shared with me that some of the other dancers and even the coach were saying negative things about her.

She would often come home from practice crying. As the spring show grew closer, we talked a lot about finishing what you start. When you begin something, you should not quit…unless. That word "unless" holds a lot of meaning. Going to dance every day became an emotional struggle for her, and after several discussions with the coach, I decided to pull her from the team.

The decision did not come lightly. I struggled with what kind of message I was sending; what I was allowing my daughter to believe. I did not want her to believe when things get hard, it's okay to quit. On the other hand, I wanted to teach her if someone is mistreating her, it is time to take appropriate protective action.

Unless. That word kept sticking in my head, and I decided to talk with my daughter.

Pulling my daughter into my bedroom just days before her big spring show, I told her: "I am pulling you from this dance company. It is my decision as your mom. I am doing this to protect your emotional health. This team has become an unhealthy place for you, and my job as your mom is to protect you. This was a good situation until it was not. Pulling you from this team is not about allowing you to quit; rather, it is about sticking up for you when someone is mistreating you. It's not often that I decide without your input, but in this situation, I am going to."

I approached my daughter this way to help release any guilt she might carry over quitting the team. She knew people were mistreating her. She knew I did not allow her to quit things once she started. And most importantly, she now knows if someone is mistreating her, it's okay to make a change.

The light bulb of empowerment protects. Protection is a part of empowerment. It means you have set healthy boundaries, and if those boundaries are crossed, you are ready to take appropriate action based on the situation. Protection is not always an easy choice to implement, but it is one that empowerment often requires.

EMPOWERMENT OF PATIENCE

Patience is a great source of empowerment, and there are many ways to practice this trait. Empowerment of patience occurs when there is a lot to say or do, but limited resources, such as limited time or space to talk. In one meeting, I remember watching a colleague exhibit vast patience with the person leading the meeting. The leader was energetically making his case for some ideas the group members were obviously not fans of. My colleague, instead of blurting out his ideas, patiently waited and listened to the leader's thoughts.

When the leader had finally said all he needed to, he asked for feedback from the group. My colleague continued to sit silently while others shared their ideas. He quietly nodded his head, showing understanding and active listening skills. Eventually, my colleague spoke up and shared some great ideas about the topic at hand.

Observing someone I highly respected who showed a lot of grace and patience to the leader of the meeting taught me a valuable lesson. When you listen, you learn more than when you talk. My colleague's approach of listening first and then speaking gave him a great advantage. Taking this approach allowed him to hear everyone's ideas and present his idea in the best way possible. I still remember how this gentleman presented himself in the meeting, and to this day, it encourages me to be more of a listener than a talker.

EMPOWERMENT OF DECISION

On any given day, you make thousands of decisions. Decisions like what you are going to wear, what you will eat for each meal, how you are going to spend your free time, what roads to take to your destination, whom to spend time with, how you spend your money, and so on. When faced with any situation where you must decide what to do, you can either choose to be proactive or reactive.

Proactive decisions can make your day feel lighter. These are decisions you make in advance, such as planning your schedule for the following day before you go to bed at night. You might make a meal plan for the next week instead of deciding what to eat for dinner thirty minutes before dinnertime. Even making a grocery list before you go to the store is a proactive decision. Decisions like these help pave the way for a smoother journey. This is not to say that occasional detours won't come along because, of course, they do. But when you have a plan, it gives your brain room to focus on the more important decisions. A plan allows you to hit the ground running each morning instead of using your "brain juices" to think about what you want to accomplish that day—because you already know!

Reactive decisions are decisions you make in the spur of the moment in reaction to another variable that has just been added to the mix. The thing about decisions is the more you make them, the better you get at making them. When you need to make a reactive decision, make your absolute best guess and then move on. When you see the results of that decision, reflect on the decision, what happened because of that decision, and move forward. Reflection is important. It is how you sharpen your decision-making skills.

You will get it wrong sometimes, especially when you must make a reactive decision. When you get it wrong, you earn the opportunity to reflect. Take that opportunity, learn, and grow from it, and then do better. The world does not expect you to be perfect; it just expects you to try your best.

EMPOWERMENT OF NEGOTIATION

I have always loved parents who allow their children some space, when appropriate, to challenge what their parents say or do. Parents who operate with: "It is my way or the highway," or expect their kids to obey commands the first time have never been my cup of tea. Same goes for the boss-employee relationship. My favorite employees are the people who respectfully challenge my opinion when we are brainstorming or in a staff meeting. These are great people to have by your side because they help you expand your thinking by presenting ideas you would not have thought of on your own.

The thing about taking this approach is we never know how to do it best, but if we listen to others, we can learn how to do it better. If we instruct our kids, our employees, and those we mentor to challenge what we say, the conversation grows richer, and everyone gains insight. Of course, when I encourage people to take this approach, I encourage them to be respectful in their challenge. It is not only about challenging, but doing it in a way that feels collaborative and respectful to all involved.

Perfect is probably impossible, but "better" is usually within reach. The only way others are going to speak up and present their ideas is if we, as the leader, create a collaborative environment where others feel their opinions and ideas are valued. This is true of children, employees, partners, friends—basically everyone.

When you feel your opinion is valued, you are more comfortable speaking up. I want my employees and children alike to embrace the anxiety that sometimes comes with speaking up and do it anyway. By setting up this kind of environment, my hope is they feel they can negotiate and bring in innovative ideas. I do my best to listen. Sometimes I go with their idea, and other times, I don't. As a leader, it is vital to set a tone that ensures those who look up to you feel what they have to say is important to you.

When working with a leader, it is valuable to embrace the anxiety that comes with your ideas and begin to get comfortable speaking up. Embrace the anxiety and do it anyway. Remember, if you are speaking up, do it respectfully. Do not interrupt. Wait for the right time to share your ideas. And then go for it!

EMPOWERMENT OF LETTING GO

Letting go is an empowering and sometimes heart-tugging decision.

How you decide it is time to let go is up to you. The act of letting go, as difficult as it is, empowers you. When the time comes to say goodbye to a relationship, friendship, job, house, etc., a mixed bag of emotions will come along with you in that journey. That is expected, normal, and part of the process of saying goodbye to anything.

No one can convince you when the right time to let go is. No one can do it for you, but when the time is right, you will know. You will experience "a moment." In that moment, you will find clarity and new thoughts that create confidence in your decision to let go. Of course, confidence is not the only emotion you will feel. I tell clients they can feel a rainbow of emotions at any given time. Sometimes these emotions may seem to conflict with each other, but both can be true at the same time.

Conflicting emotions can be confusing since it may seem like you can only choose one. Just know that more than one can be true at the same time. Experiencing conflicting emotions when you are going through the journey of letting go is okay. Tell yourself it is okay.

Sometimes letting go is forced upon you like when you lose a job, a loved one, or a relationship. When the choice is made for you, it may hurt, but the pain will eventually fade. It may not feel like a journey of empowerment, and the hurt may seem endless, but it will end. In this kind of journey, the empowerment of letting go will be more of an emotional journey, reconciling with the events that led to the loss you experienced. This life transition might lead you to believe you have lost control or lost your power. You might even feel you lost some self-worth, but the journey of empowerment will be your guide. You may feel down now, but trust that it won't last forever. Process the difficult emotions.

The empowerment of letting go does not mean forgetting, especially in the case of grief—which we will discuss later. People often say, "Forgive and forget." I don't buy into this approach. When you forgive, you are cutting the ties that are still causing you pain, but you do not have to forget. If your journey of empowerment through letting go deals with mistreatment, you can forgive when you are ready, but that does not mean you forget. You don't have to let your boundaries down and open yourself up to repeated hurt. The act of forgiving does not have to be accompanied by forgetting unless you want that element to be included. You can still experience the same kind of healing whether or not you forget. That is what is empowering. It is up to you to decide what is best for you. You take your best guess, and if it works out, great. If not, try again.

SUMMARY

Protection, patience, decision making, negotiation, and letting go are five strengths to help build your light bulb of empowerment. Each can cause emotions as you engage with it, and each offers you a different power. No one starts out being fantastic at all of them, but you may find some are easier than others. Recognize the ones that come easily to you as your strengths, lean on them, and use them when appropriate. Work on building the empowerments you may be weakest in by using them. The more you use them, the stronger you will make them, and they will become easier to use in the future.

Empowerments will keep you on track when you are working toward a goal. They will give you encouragement and help you believe you can make it to the finish line. They will show you where your strengths are and help you get to the end. Set goals and lean on empowerments to help you achieve what you want. Though you may carry broken pieces with you, you can still find peace. Keep going. Keep moving closer to your goals. Keep your eyes and heart focused on the things you know will help lead you to more peace. Continue to seek the peace among your pieces.

Chapter 15

THE LIGHT BULB OF SERVICE

"Opportunity is missed by most people because it is dressed in overalls and looks like work."

— Thomas Edison,
Inventor of the Filament Inside the Light Bulb

Getting your light to shine not only happens through investing in yourself and your personal growth, but also through helping others grow their light. Investing in and strengthening another's light has a serendipitous effect on your own light. As you take part in strengthening another's light, you will feel your light getting brighter. It is the best feeling in the world! One of the most sacred experiences is helping another's light grow brighter. This is when the world grows stronger. Sharing your knowledge, experience, and love with another is one of the greatest experiences, and serendipitously, it makes your light brighter.

Many forms of service are available to participate in if you are not already doing so. You can serve by offering a small compliment to someone walking, or by volunteering to help a larger organization. The key to experiencing the serendipitous effect of the light of service is to offer yourself and your service.

People can be hesitant to engage in service, thinking they don't have much to give (time, knowledge, etc.), but that is the darkness imposing doubts in their mind. The more you get involved, the more you will benefit from serving. Self-doubt is only the darkness trying to squelch your light of service. You do not need a special skill to help others. The more you help, the more light you put into the world. Investing in the light around you grows everyone involved, including yourself.

INVESTMENT IN YOURSELF

Think back to a time when someone made a real difference in your life. Think about what they did to make that difference. Did they invest extra time with you? Did they go above and beyond their job for you? Did they show you compassion in a time of need? Without these kinds of people, you would not be where you are today.

Just like the light bulb starts out whole and gets damaged through life's journey, you may find yourself thinking about someone who tried to soften the damage the world brought you. Sometimes you will serve, and other times, you will receive service. Many have an easier time giving than receiving. If you experience this, you are not alone—you will have seasons of giving and receiving.

When it is your time to receive, allow yourself to be served. You may need that act of kindness, and allowing people the opportunity to serve is also a blessing to them. They benefit from helping you just as you benefit from helping them. For most people, it is difficult to be served, and you are probably no exception. The person choosing to serve you is showing their love. This is how love grows. When you allow someone to serve you, your relationship will grow, and when you see a need in them and serve them, your relationship will grow again. No one wants to be in a relationship where acts of kindness only go one way. In addition to that, you are worth their time. You are worth their effort. You are worth their energy.

BARRIERS

One of the biggest barriers to allowing ourselves to be served is wanting to avoid putting another in a bind. Remember this—when someone asks if they can help, they are really asking if they can help.

If you need help, let them help. It may be difficult for you, but allow it anyway. Difficult is okay. Growth happens in difficulty. Letting someone help not only strengthens you in accepting the offer, but strengthens your relationship with that person.

When someone wants to invest in you, remember the people you invested in and how that felt to you. Did you feel hesitant? Probably not. Allow those who want to invest in you to invest in you.

A WORD OF CAUTION

Sometimes the act of service will not be genuine and service will be offered out of obligation, either on your side to another or from another to you. This can happen when family or relationship bonds trump desire. When this happens, you must decide where to set your personal boundaries about offering and accepting service. This is quite different than a genuine offer to serve or be served. When this happens, make sure you are not opening yourself up to more pain.

How do you know when you should set boundaries about accepting and offering service? There is no cookie-cutter advice other than encouraging you to listen to your thoughts. Listen to the uncertainty and possible anxiety that come to mind. Might accepting/giving in this way create a situation that will cause emotional or physical harm to you or someone you love? In this self-reflection, you may find the answer to whether you should engage in offering/accepting the service.

Watch out for light stealers. Be careful of those who would come alongside you allegedly to strengthen your dim light but who really want to steal the last bit of light you have. Some will present themselves as light givers who are really light stealers. It can be difficult to identify these people at first, but in time, you will notice something feels off. You will notice things they say cause you to give more of your light than you have. They will tell you they have light to give, but then never share their light with you. You may even feel exhausted after spending time with them. Be careful when you encounter these light stealers disguised as those who want to serve. As you continue your journey of strengthening your and others' light, your discernment and objectivity will grow, and you will more quickly be to able identify, set, and maintain boundaries with those who take away from your light.

INVESTMENT IN OTHERS

Investing in others is so much fun—and some work! Obviously, you can invest in others on your own, or you can go for it with others and turn your investment into a group activity. So many ways to invest in others exist through organizations like Big Brothers Big Sisters, Angel Tree, and other non-profits. These are organizational acts of service. Other individual investments could be something as small as helping someone carry in their groceries, helping another with household tasks, or even sending a card of encouragement.

One of my favorite ways to invest in other people through acts of service is to hold space for them. In this way, I allow them room to talk, process, and reflect on whatever they are going through. As a professional counselor, I found early on that allowing myself to be of service in this way came easy to me.

I first realized this inner strength when I was in grade school. I was at a birthday party, and I noticed one of my friends was sitting away from the group and looked sad. We were at a roller-skating rink in Portland, Oregon, so I decided to roll on over and talk to her. She did not want to talk, so I just sat by her. This memory, though not a major event, has stuck in my thoughts over the years, and it is the first time I went out of my way to care for another person. This started my journey to realizing that helping people was something I value, so I began to grow that skill within myself.

More recently, I went swimming at a gym one day—I was going often to get in shape—and when I went in to change clothes, an older woman was sitting on the bench in the bathroom with tears in her eyes. I softly leaned over to her and gently asked if she was okay. She nodded and said she was. I asked if I could do anything to help her, and she said no. Then I asked if I could just sit beside her, to which she agreed. I sat beside her in silence for about ten minutes.

Sometimes being with another person's pain is more important than what you had planned for yourself. I think back to the stories of Mother Teresa and how she approached others. The stories of her sitting with people in their pain are many. After a couple of minutes had passed, this woman turned and thanked me, and we went on our way. She did not tell me what was going on that was causing her pain, and I did not ask.

A couple of weeks later, I was back at the gym when I crossed paths with this same woman. We were in the pool, and rather than ask her about the situation, I chose to give her space. Giving space in this way empowers the other person to engage or distance themselves as they choose. Giving space this way can be just as important as engaging. The woman swam up to me and asked if I remembered her. I told her I did, and she thanked me for sitting with her. She told me about the situation that had caused her pain, and I listened.

Investing in others can be through intentional acts of service, or through unplanned acts of caring that happen in the moment. These are my favorite acts of service. The next time you find yourself in a moment like this, see what happens when you embrace the opportunity to care for another. Do not try to lead the moment; just be there and let it play out. Hold space for the moment. Give space to the other person's emotions and thoughts. Be patient. Sometimes the best support is offering another the gift of your company through your silent presence.

INVESTMENT IN GROUPS

Group investment in service can be just as fun as an individual investment, though it takes a bit more work and planning. Investing with a group can come through your local food pantry, church, non-profit, or other organization. If you are interested in spreading your light through group service, from this point on consider yourself the "point person." The point person organizes the group service.

As the point person, you can decide to volunteer at a large organization or to get a group of friends, family, or colleagues together to volunteer where you see fit. If you are organizing a group to volunteer at an organization, you will need to choose a place, set a time, and arrange the logistics of the event for the group.

Shining your light by inviting others to join you in a group volunteer opportunity helps spread the support across many individuals. This is a terrific way to make your light grow through service. Many people choose the holidays to organize a group effort, but I encourage you to think of other times to volunteer as well.

Just like in individual service, with group service, you will feel your light grow. This is the way you were made. When you give your service to another, you will notice good feelings inside. Some credit the hormone oxytocin for this good feeling. Oxytocin is released when you are hugging someone you love. It is the hormone released during intimacy, and it can be released through doing good acts for others. This is the "feel good hormone."

THE STRENGTH IN THE DIM LIGHT

Isn't it interesting that to change a light bulb, you need light? It would be difficult to change a burned-out light bulb in the dark. You could go at it alone using your hands and fingers to help guide you, but having additional light to accomplish the task sure makes it a lot easier.

Just like changing a light bulb requires light, no one can get through this world alone. At times you will find yourself needing help. You also will find opportunities to serve. Again, serving for most comes easier than receiving. We know this to be true. Challenge yourself not only to serve but to embrace the times when you need service. When another person offers to serve you in a way that will help your light grow, do not decline. Challenge yourself to accept that gift of light, because it not only helps you grow, but everyone's light gets brighter.

Light bulb gifts are for everyone, and you are no exception. Sometimes you will help others' light grow, and sometimes your light will be grown by others. It can be difficult to accept, but embrace it when others offer to help grow your light. You may feel vulnerable, and even exposed. But the help and strength that comes from accepting those gifts of service can be so valuable to the light you carry. Embrace the help you are offered, especially when your light feels dim. It not only helps you, but it allows the other person the opportunity to serve.

If you find yourself trying to change a metaphorical light bulb in the dark, it can be valuable to reach out and ask for help. Asking for help is even more difficult than accepting it. When your light is dim, take that last bit of light, take that last little bit of internal strength you carry within you, and reach out to ask for help. During these times, you may be fragile, but by asking for help, your light will grow stronger. You will find that you may have to advocate for what you need when your light is dim. That is the healthy thing to do! If you find yourself struggling right now and your light is dim, reach out to those you know you can trust. Reach out to those who have earned the right to come alongside and offer you light.

SUMMARY

No light ever shines on its own forever. You need others to help strengthen your light when it feels dim, and others need the strength of your light when theirs feels dim. Taking this approach makes the entire world brighter. The more light you share, the more you have to share. Sharing your light makes you stronger. The more light you accept, the stronger you get. Having the brightest light involves both sharing your light and accepting others' gifts of light. Sharing and receiving light may not come naturally to you. It can be something you work at and strengthen. Sharing and receiving light requires boundaries as you need an element of protection for your light. Your light is valuable. Your light is worthy. Your light is worthwhile.

Section 5

IDENTIFYING LIFE TRANSITIONS

"One thing that makes it possible to be an optimist is if you have a contingency plan for when all hell breaks loose."

— Randy Pausch,
The Last Lecture

Chapter 16

THE LIGHT OF RELATIONSHIP

"To get the full value of joy you must have someone to divide it with."

— Mark Twain,
American Author and Friend of Nikola Tesla

The light bulb as it relates to intimate relationships can be complex. You can choose to give, receive, and experience this light within the relational unit. The light expands when you choose to partner with someone through connection, intimacy, and trust. Mistreatment can cause this incredibly special shared light to dim. The connection of two lights can be a very intimate experience.

Can you think of a time when you crossed paths with someone and felt the exchange of energy almost immediately? When your energy mixes with another's, you can often feel the change, or charge, as it may be, in your space. Sometimes the energy is positive and uplifting, sometimes it can be neutral, and sometimes it can be negative.

In these interactions, your light bulb either grows brighter, dims, or stays the same. Every person you interact with has a positive, negative, or neutral effect on your light. Going back to our discussion of introverts and extroverts, the quadrant (introvert, extrovert, introverted extrovert, or extroverted introvert) you identified yourself as will inform how you exchange light with others.

In everyday life, your light can sustain interactions, but when it comes to closer relationships, it is important to be more intentional about whom you choose to exchange your light with. Some you choose to share light with will protect it with their own and others will not.

In the same way, people who want to invest their light in you will come into your life, and it is up to you to choose how you want to protect their light. Remember, when someone chooses to share their light with you, it is a sacred act of authenticity and vulnerability on their part, so be careful with those who choose to share their light with you.

This topic may be taking you back to people who were not careful with the light you shared with them. It is normal to remember these times. It is painful when someone chooses to share their light and the recipient is not careful with that gift. If you are among the many who can relate to this experience, you can find healing. Your light can be healed. If you feel your light has been dimmed by another, you can heal and your light can regain its full brightness.

As you read this chapter, use it as a time of healing and explore your heart. Like the light bulb can get hurt on the path to brightness, you might look back on your relational life and identify times when you also received some scratches. When you reflect, you can choose to embrace the brokenness you carried with you. Let this chapter be about healing. Feel the embrace as this chapter helps your light shine brighter and heal the parts that have been hurt or broken by others.

OPENING YOUR HEART

The light bulb that shines within relationships first needs a place to grow. If your heart is not open to a relationship, that light will not grow. That is not to say your heart should always be open to new partners if you are not already in a relationship or desire to be. Sometimes you will want to remain single and strengthen your light through that journey. You may not be interested in partnering at all. However, if you are looking to build a relationship and strengthen its light, you can only do so if your heart and energy are open to another's light, combining their energy with yours.

A note specifically for single friends: You don't need to partner unless you want to. If your heart does not desire a partner, do not force yourself into a relationship because others tell you it is good for you. Don't force yourself into a relationship for any reason. We have a lot of reasons to partner and a lot of reasons to stay single. One option is not better than the other. You are wholly you either way.

On that note, it is not good to partner unless you feel whole as a person. Once you feel whole and have the desire to partner, look for another who also feels whole and desires a partner. One reason relationships do not work is because one person is using the other as a therapist, parent, or healer. Yes, relationships can come with these benefits, but they should not be the primary goal or focus. Being in a relationship should come from a desire to share life, not to find someone to serve your needs.

But what if you do not currently feel whole? Honestly, no one is ever fully whole. If you want to get stronger and work toward wholeness, search for wholeness. You can do this through energy healing, professional counseling, therapy, reiki, or any path you feel called to that will result in making your light healthier. Getting closer to individual wholeness includes taking the path of healing you feel called to. If you are carrying recent pain, it may not be the best time to partner. If you have recently been through a divorce, breakup, or trauma, adding a new relationship into the mix may detract from your healing journey.

Having an open heart is important to finding the motivation to partner. Partnering should not be based on obligation, rebounding, or boredom. Having an open heart comes from having done work on yourself, being stable in the world, and experiencing the desire to share your world with another. If you are not in that place, do not partner until you can go to them the way you want them to come to you. You do not have to be perfect and should not be looking for someone who is perfect, but you need to be able to offer your care for them, and they should be able to offer their care for you, each in a healthy way.

FINDING THE RIGHT FIT

So, how do you find the right fit to help you experience the best possible success in your relationship? The first step is making sure you know yourself. By learning who you are, you will also learn what fits you best.

You can start discovering the kind of person you want to be with when you know the kind of person you are. Who you are speaks directly to the kind of person you should look for to partner with. In the helping professions, we know partners with similar beliefs, interests, passions, and goals do better in relationships. This is not to say you must line up completely, or that some couples with completely opposing views are not living their best lives with each other. But generally speaking, if you are looking for a partner, it is helpful if they share your ideals and interests.

Another thing to consider is whether you want to date casually or are looking for a long-term relationship. Looking for someone to date can, at times, be more about having fun. Looking for a long-term relationship can be more about finding a life partner. Ask yourself what your intentions are. Knowing and understanding what you are looking for will help guide you to a partner who is looking for a similar type of relationship.

ACTIVITY

Take five minutes to complete the following activity. Take out a piece of paper and write down your top ten life priorities. What is most important to you? How do you spend most of your time? How do you prefer to spend most of your time? What kinds of things do you like to invest in? How do you want to interact with your family and extended family?

Next, write out your top ten life goals. What do you hope to accomplish in the next five, ten, and twenty years? What do you want to do? Where would you like to visit? How do you want to raise your kids? Do you want kids?

It will be easier to find the right partner if you look for someone who respects and even enhances the qualities you listed. Keep this list in a special place and refer to it as you look for a partner.

THE THREE PHASES

If you are already in a relationship, hopefully you are growing together. Every relationship goes through many distinct stages, but the primary three seem to be the honeymoon phase, the middle phase, and the long-term phase. Each of these phases has its own characteristics that help you grow together or identify areas in the relationship that need work.

The honeymoon phase is exactly what it sounds like—when two people have recently partnered and decide they want to be together. In this phase, everything feels amazing and new. Excitement and anticipation are high and you feel incredible. Most likely, you are both enjoying and exploring each other. You learn a lot in this stage.

In the honeymoon stage, even if you knew each other before, you are getting to know each other in a whole new way as partners. You are learning about the relationship and how you work together as a pair. Fun and adventure is all around you during the honeymoon phase.

Next comes the middle phase. The foundational connection you made in the honeymoon phase is full of fun memories, and your interest and connection is apparent. The primary difference in the middle phase is you begin and continue to see your partner's faults. Difficulties may bubble to the surface. This is when the "realness" of the partnership comes to the surface and is evaluated.

In the middle phase, partners ask themselves if they want to continue the relationship after learning more about the other. This information did not come out in the honeymoon phase; it only comes out in the middle phase. This is when you start to notice how your partner chews their food, manages their finances, or invests in those around them. This is the phase where all the intricacies and eccentricities come to light and you decide if you want to continue the relationship.

If you find you want to stay with your partner after seeing who they really are, congratulations. You have entered the last relationship phase—the long-term phase. This is the most exciting phase, though you might be thinking that would be the honeymoon phase. The honeymoon phase is fun and exciting, but the long-term phase is deep and full of real intimacy and connection. This last stage consists of everything real and authentic. You have seen the good. You have experienced the bad. And in all of that, you have chosen each other. You have decided your partner is worth the effort, even after seeing all their idiosyncrasies that annoy you and they have seen yours.

THE BUCKETS YOU CARRY

The metaphorical bucket comes into play in this last phase. Everyone living carries two buckets. One bucket is filled with everything good they have to offer a partner and the world. The other is filled with everything else: their struggles, annoying habits, vices, etc. When deciding to date, keep in mind everyone has a bucket of good and a bucket of bad.

People try to hide their bucket of bad and only show their bucket of good. Seeing only the good in another can lead to temptation. When your relationship struggles, if you or your partner starts to admire another's good bucket, you or they may be tempted. In this dynamic, the new person's bucket of bad, their shortcomings, are hidden. For instance, when one partner decides to have an affair, the new person is only showing their good bucket. In this case, the honeymoon phase is brought back, but only for one of the partners, the one going outside the partnership.

The excitement of this new honeymoon phase can blind a partner to the new person's bad bucket and the light in the relationship with their partner. In an affair, one may think they are trading a bucket of bad for a new bucket of good, but that is not the case. They are just trading one set of buckets for another, and the shortfalls will be revealed when the new relationship hits the second phase.

If you are partnered and not finding the relationship as fulfilling as you did in the past, before you decide to leave, think about what attracted you to your partner in the first place. What changed? Then ask yourself if it is worth trading their buckets for someone else's buckets. Sometimes the answer is yes, it is worth walking away from the good and bad of your partner because the relationship is just too unhealthy. And sometimes the relationship can recover by accessing various kinds of internal and external assistance methods.

PROPER MAINTENANCE

With the foundation of the relationship established and an understanding of the phase you are in, maintenance is the next big task. Any light will dim without proper maintenance. The same is true for the light in relationships. Once you stop investing in a relationship, your connection will shrink or dim. Investing in your relationship is of utmost importance. It is not about being tough. Investment in your relationship should come from a soft and eager *heart desire* to continue the connection you felt during the honeymoon phase.

Continuing the honeymoon phase connection into the long-term phase can be tricky, but it can be done with ease through some intentionality.

Investing takes time, effort, and sometimes money. Just like with anything you invest in, these things are needed for growth. Never stop investing in your partner. Never stop investing intentional care, surprise, and connection in the relationship. These are things that make your light bulb as a couple shine!

How is maintenance done? First, plan regular date nights. Are you poor college students or young parents? No problem. Plan a picnic, go for a walk, look up local free concerts, find free or inexpensive things to do together. Making memories brings opportunities for connection to grow. You can't make memories sitting around the house. Making memories must be intentional. You do not want to have good intentions and poor follow-through when it comes to investing in your relationship. Being lazy will end in a lost connection later.

If you have the time, set specific date nights for each week. If you are busy and unable to set a weekly date night, try every other week. At a bare minimum, go out once a month. A fun and collaborative approach to date nights is to have partners rotate planning it. One partner plans a date during the odd months of the year. The other partner plans a date on the even months in the year. This allows each to plan at least six dates per year. Intentionally make time for at least the bare minimum. Your relationship is important; invest time in it and in each other so your connection does not fade.

AUTONOMY

Just as proper maintenance is important, so too is maintaining your own personhood, and individuality. Maintaining who you are as a whole person inside and outside of the relationship makes your partnership better and richer. By continuing to invest in yourself, you remain whole and continue to add light to your relationship. You can do this through hobbies, interests, and/or friends. These, of course, can be shared with your partner, but they should also be invested in on your own.

You do not want to end up with a lopsided relationship where your partner becomes your entire world. When I see relationships like this in counseling sessions, I usually see one partner having a lot of control over the other, which is not a sign of a healthy relationship. To have a great partnership, you must invest in outside relationships. Spending time with people who can relate to you and your experiences is helpful, which often means women spending time with women and men spending time with men, since you share similar upbringings, social norms, physiology, etc. But any healthy, platonic relationship can be fulfilling.

Maintaining autonomy as a crucial element in your personhood and relationship keeps your individual light bright and brightens the light of your couplehood. This is valuable, especially when your partner's light dims—then they can lean on your bright light to help strengthen theirs and vice-versa..

A quick word of caution here: Leaning on your partner's light should be only a "sometimes event." It should not happen "all the time." Sometimes it is good to glean light from your partner to stay strong, but your partner's light should not be key to your autonomy. You should not need your partner's light to know who you are. If you do, you may start to feel you have lost yourself and forget who you really are.

Ensuring your light is strong to maintain your sense of autonomy while partnered is a smart decision. Hopefully, you will partner with someone who takes the same stance. Codependency grows when the partnership is out of balance. Make sure you are not draining your partner's light. Overall, protect your light, protect your partner's light, and protect the relationship's light. When you protect all three, and maintain their balance, you should end up with a healthy relationship.

SUMMARY

The light that comes from a relationship is complex, rewarding, and requires a lot of investment and work. So much intimacy happens in the light of healthy relationships. Whether you are single, newly partnered, or in a long-term relationship, being intentional about your relationship's light is important. In every stage, what you do will dim or brighten the light you have to give and the light you receive.

Continue to make good choices because that is where the light of relationship gets its power. When and if you are partnered, continue to make good choices for your partner, thinking not only of yourself but of them as well. Too often, we forget our individual choices matter to our partner. Bring your partner along on the journey you are taking. And allow yourself to be brought along on their journey. As Mark Twain said, "When love is shared, you will be able to receive the full experience of it."

Experiencing partnership, true and genuine, is the best experience in the world, but only if you do not sell yourself short.

Chapter 17

THE LIGHT OF PARENTING

"For anything worth having one must pay the price; and the price is always work, patience, love, self-sacrifice."

— John Burroughs,
American Naturalist

The instant my daughter was born, my life changed forever. I became a parent. A mom. From this point on, no matter where I was, with her or not, I carried her with me in my heart. I was proud to be a mom, but also confused, anxious, and concerned, along with all the other emotions new parents experience. I was not sure how to "mom."

Then, a couple of years later, I had my son, and my daughter became a sibling. Being a mother of two brought joy and challenges, but I knew I was up to the task of learning how to become the best parent I could be. To this day, I am most proud of being Mom and how I parent my two sweet kids.

If you are a parent, thinking about becoming a parent, or have a parent, you have seen the changing dynamics life brings into the parent-child relationship. Parenting can be just as rewarding as it is conflicting. Keep one important aspect in mind when approaching the "how to" of parenting. You are either learning "how to parent" or "how not to parent" when you see other people's approaches.

The light bulb as it relates to parenting includes the goal of raising healthy, compassionate, empathetic, responsible children. Parenting, as everyone says, is the most rewarding and challenging task you will ever undertake. Just like in adult relationships, children need intentional time focused on them and their growth. Parents should consider themselves as mentors to their children, providing strength, a healthy foundation, and love.

Some children do not receive the parenting they deserve. If you are among them, even as an adult, know that you are not alone. Know that you can be a different kind of parent to your children than what you experienced when you were younger. If you are an aunt, uncle, or mentor to a child or children, this chapter applies to you as well. This chapter is just dipping your toes into parenting advice. If you are looking for more information, I highly recommend *Parenting with Love and Logic* by Jim Fay and Foster Cline.

KEEPING YOUR CHILDREN'S LIGHTS BRIGHT

The first thing to consider when thinking about how the light bulb effect relates to children is making sure you do not burn out your kids' light. How can you avoid doing this? By having patience, listening without interrupting, setting and maintaining healthy boundaries and rules, and caring about the things they care about. Taking an interest in your children and the things that interest them is really validating for your children. If your child likes Lego, spending time building stuff with them could feed their heart. If your child likes reading, taking them to a bookstore to pick out a new book could feed their heart. Feeding your child/children's hearts with positive, loving intentional actions will help build your bond and keep their light bright.

Avoid exacerbating your children while trying to help keep their light bright. You will no doubt get into arguments with your children, and it is up to you to decide if it is time to take a break from the situation. Your five-year-old, your thirteen-year-old, and even your sixteen-year-old will not always know when they need a break in the conversation. Exacerbation happens when one or more people in the conversation get overwhelmed. When this happens, it is time to give them space. You can approach this in many healthy ways.

In any conflict with your child, when the situation has become too heated, a break is helpful. When you decide to call for a break, make sure you include a time limit. For instance, you could tell them you would like to take a fifteen-minute break. This tells your child you are not walking away from them; instead, you are walking away from the situation. This helps prevent feelings of abandonment because you are telling them when you will be back to continue to work out the situation. This is especially important: If you tell your child you will be back in fifteen minutes, be back in fifteen minutes! If they are not ready to talk at that point, it's okay. You can give them another ten minutes, and then, of course, go back at the end of that ten minutes.

With children, communication is key. The way you say what you say, the tone of voice, the volume, and the words you choose are all important. In times of conflict, the way you treat your child is the way you are teaching them to treat others. How you approach conflict with your kids is not just about approaching the conflict; it is also what I like to call a mentoring moment or a teachable moment.

Mentoring and teachable moments are windows of opportunity for teaching our kids. In those moments, you are teaching them either by your behavior, by taking an interest and asking questions, or by the experience you are exposing them to. The window of a teachable moment is not always open. It opens when your child is interested and you recognize the opportunity to incorporate a little mentoring. Look for these important moments to help maintain your child's light.

JURASSIC PARK'S LIGHT OF TRUTH

If you have a toddler or teenager, you may experience a lot of boundary pushing—it's a natural part of development, and your child needs to do it to learn about the world. I often tell my kids when they are being sassy that it is their job as teenagers to push the boundaries. It's how they learn about the world, where the rules start and stop, and how they are enforced. I also like to give them a compliment, telling them they are doing an excellent job of pushing their boundaries. This helps lighten the mood when the tension is high. We all have a little laugh about them doing their job of pushing boundaries wonderfully. This also shows them conflict within a family is normal, appropriate, and will be worked out in a healthy way.

Then I tell my kids what my job as a mom is. I say my job is to maintain the boundaries, and I need to do a good job too. So, I tell them to do a good job pushing boundaries, and I will do a good job maintaining boundaries, and our house will be balanced.

I do not recommend, nor do I use, an authoritarian approach. I encourage my kids to question my decisions and the world around them because when they do, the precious windows of opportunity for teachable moments open. I also want them to know it is appropriate to question authority, and if any adult makes them uncomfortable or they feel the person may cause them harm, they do not have to comply with the adult.

We also often talk about respect and the balance between respecting adults and having the freedom to question them, which can be tricky. To protect our children from adults who might prey on them, we must allow them to ask questions. Asking "why" is vastly different than rebelling against rules set by legitimate authority figures in appropriate settings.

Children are a lot like the dinosaurs in *Jurassic Park* that kept testing the electric fence even though they got shocked in order to find the weak part in the fence. The dinosaurs would test and test until they came upon a weak point, and then they would go through that weak point. Your job as a parent and/or mentor is to be the fence. When your children test you, as they will since that is a part of their job and developmental journey, your job is to be the strong fence and hold the boundary so they can learn about the world around them, including how rules and boundaries are set, maintained, and enforced.

INVESTING IN YOUR CHILD'S LIGHT

While maintaining your own light, it is also very important to nurture, invest in, and teach your children and those you mentor how to invest in and maintain their own light. Investment and maintenance of one's light are two separate actions. Investment is the work one puts into ensuring their light is bright, whereas maintenance is ensuring the light stays bright so the dark does not get in to dim the light. Both are equally important to you and those you influence, especially your children.

You can invest in your child's light in many ways. And your intentionality drives a lot of your investment. When you are intentional about the positive and constructive things you say to your children, you are guiding their path and investing in their light. When you take an interest in something your children like, especially if you might not like that same thing, that is an investment in your child's light. When you set and keep healthy rules to ensure they do not fall into the darkness, that is also an investment in their light. The cliché that being a parent is difficult is so true, but the powers that be have entrusted you with this little soul, and it is up to you to make sure you raise them to be responsible and caring adults.

Maintaining your child's light is a bit different than investing in it, because maintaining consists of watching and making sure your little (or not so little) one's brightness keeps growing and they do not backslide and start to dim or go dark. This level of awareness takes a lot of quiet observation. We know children don't like it when we tell them what to do, even though we have to do that a lot. Anytime you can gently guide your child in the right direction when you notice their light changing is fantastic!

Observation is key to maintenance. You have to know when your child's light changes, when it shifts, and when it might be in trouble. The best way to do this is to know and understand what your child's light looks like when it is bright and healthy. You learn this through observing your child's everyday life. This might sound basic, as if every parent would and should be doing this, but not every parent does.

You need to know early when your child's light starts to dim so you can help them. As a parent, you may see your child withdrawing from things they normally like. In those moments, you will decide what action to take to help keep their light bright. Sometimes that means giving them space to think through the situation they are in. Sometimes it means having an open and honest conversation about what is going on using your best listening skills.

Don't interrupt when they are sharing. This is super-important to keep in mind as you engage them in conversation. When our children talk, if we interrupt, they will likely share less than they would have if we listened for a couple of more seconds. The five-second rule is helpful. Just wait a full five seconds after they stop talking before you start.

If you use the five-second rule, you may find they will continue to share even more, and you will learn more about the situation and about your child. In waiting five seconds and learning more, you will better find out about how you can help them get through whatever it is they are sharing about.

When speaking to your child and using your best listening skills, also try asking them if they would just like you to listen or if they would like you to give them feedback. You might be surprised by how often they just want you to be a stronger light and provide space for them to share. By just listening, you validate their ability to solve their dim light situation. Children like to vent just like adults. On that note, adults, for the most part, love to help children, so wanting to offer advice is understandable when your child comes to you about a situation they are thinking through. *But*, just like adults, children sometimes do not feel the need for advice and just want the space to share and connect. As a parent, make sure you are a good listener. Once you have built a good communicative relationship with your child and they know you will actively listen, use the five-second rule, and support their light when they want to share with you.

EMPOWERING YOUR CHILDREN

The next way you can help your child's light shine is by teaching them how to find the strength to maintain and grow their light. This happens when you help your child find the strength in their light as they grow older. You do not want your kids to rely on you to be their only source of light. The time will come, mostly around their teens, when they will want to start growing their light on their own. This is not to say they do not need you, but they begin to want more space. They still need you as their grounding light, but they are also finding ways to maintain and grow their light autonomously. This is a developmentally appropriate stage for them to go through.

Some ways you can show and teach your children how to grow their own light is by modeling how you do it. Children are naturally great observers, and they will watch you to see how you invest in yourself. Do you have self-care nights where you take a hot bath, light some candles, and turn some music on? Maybe you go out for a night with friends. You may even pick up a good book or watch a movie. It is important for children to see their parents as responsible adults, and it is also important for them to see their parents making self-care a priority. You can also encourage your kids to do the things you do for self-care. You could get them a bath bomb and show them how to take a relaxing bath. You could explain the importance of "chill time" and reading, or taking time to watch a good movie. You, as their parent, are also their mentor, and what you say is important to them—even when they roll their eyes!

Another way you can help your child's light grow is by encouraging them to get involved in their community. This could be through sports, school clubs, local organizations, or churches. Getting involved and rubbing shoulders with their peers in a positive environment gives them experiential activities to be a part of and feel like they belong. Again, talking about the intentionality that goes into growing and maintaining their light can greatly benefit your child as you essentially give them food for thought. What you teach them will stay with them, so teach them well.

SHINING BRIGHTLY

Modeling your bright light for your children is a positive action. To shine is being proactive with your child's confidence and instilling in them the act of being authentically who you are. Showing your children how to shine by example is a wonderful way of teaching them to embrace their bright light and the things that feed their light bulbs.

When they discover something they are good at, it is a fantastic opportunity to invest in that skill. As a parent, support their skills and let their light grow ever brighter. Proactively look for the things they are good at, but be careful not to put interests you would like them to have on them. This is where the power of observation comes in. Observe your child to learn about *their* interests and skills, and then invest in those areas. After that, let your children be proud of their unique and individual accomplishments.

Word of warning: You may want your child to get straight A's, be the quarterback, or get the lead in the play, but if they are not interested, do not push it. Make sure you invest in your child's interests, not the things you would like them to be into because you are interested in those areas. Helping your child find their own confidence will be empowering for them to experience. This approach will help them feel supported.

When your children begin to shine on their own, let them. This is a sign they are discovering their independence, and when they need help, hopefully, they will ask. Life is a good teacher, as well—although everyone has had to learn some lessons the hard way from time to time. Your children will be no exception. Give them the freedom to make mistakes, but also reassure them you will be there if they need you. Allowing age-appropriate and safe freedoms will also help them feel they can shine on their own, independently. Everyone wants freedom. Freedom through love is even better. Knowing someone is standing beside you in your freedom, in case your light starts to dim, is the best.

AVOIDING THE DAMAGE

Avoiding damage as much as possible will help minimize your children's pain. Teach them what to embrace and what to stay away from. Have you ever dripped water on a hot light bulb? If even a couple of drops are sprinkled on a hot light bulb, the glass will break. Teaching your children what to embrace to help them shine and what to avoid that will cause them pain is essential. That is not to say they will listen and always follow your advice, but when they go off script, if you have invested in their light, hopefully, if they are hurting, they will come to you for strength. This will not always happen, but you want them to know the door is always open and you will share your light.

The quote listed at the top of this chapter is so fitting for parenthood. Parents want their children to avoid as much damage as possible, but damage is part of life. Beauty can be found in damage. Damage doesn't happen to reveal beauty, but when damage is done, thankfully, someone will help you through the damage, and in that there is beauty. Your children will be hurt, but there is so much beauty in standing beside them when their light bulb is damaged. Like the quote says, parenting is also work. Parenting is love. Parenting is sacrifice. And parenting is patience. When your child's light bulb is damaged, as a parent you have the strength to help them feel supported and loved, and you can help them survive the damage. In that support, there is so much beauty.

One other way to help your children avoid damage to their light is leading by example when you fail. When you fail, demonstrate how to cope with it. Your failure is a window of opportunity to teach your kids how to apologize, to make amends, to move on, to do better next time—the lessons are endless. And all you have to do is let them see you respond well to failure.

When you fail with your children, you can make it right by genuinely admitting your mistake and offering a heartfelt apology. Apologizing is like a math equation—there are ways to do it effectively, and there are ways to do it poorly. When apologizing to your children, the first step is taking responsibility and admitting what you did. Next, ask for forgiveness. Finally, ask if you can do anything to rectify the situation and reduce the pain you caused. This shows your humility. You model a good apology and they learn how it feels, and you show it is acceptable to make mistakes and take responsibility for your actions when you do. Doing all this and setting this example shows them how to do it with others and the appropriate way to take responsibility for their actions.

A good apology might sound something like, "I am sorry I yelled at you and hurt your feelings. Will you forgive me, and what can I do to make the situation better?" Once you say this, wait for their answer. Listen to their answer. Take in what they say. Do not defend yourself. And follow through on their requests when they tell you what you can do.

A poor apology might sound something like, "I am sorry you felt I hurt your feelings." Another example would be, "I was just joking. I'm sorry you took that so seriously." The last example would be, "I am sorry that hurt you, but you…" These are poor examples of an apology because they put ownership of the offense on the hurt person, not the person who caused the injury and should take responsibility.

Words matter. What you say to your children matters. What you say to those you mentor or who look up to you matters. Words followed by actions matter even more and prove you keep your word and what you say isn't just words. With your children, following through on what you say matters most. Remember, you lead your children by example, and they need to know that when you say something, they can rely on it. Taking this approach teaches them they can depend on you, and shows them an example of how they can choose to be.

SUMMARY

Parenting is a never-ending, self-sacrificing task filled with energy, love, beauty, trials, accomplishments, and everything in between. The more intentional you are with your children in everything, the better your relationship will be. Intentionality shows itself through patience, compassion, healthy boundaries, healthy boundary enforcement, and so many other elements. Like they say, this is the most rewarding and most challenging job you will ever have, but, oh my goodness, there is nothing better than being a parent and helping a new person's light brighten, grow, and become strong. Do your best, be strong, and when you mess up, as we all do, embrace self-forgiveness.

Chapter 18

THE LIGHT OF FRIENDSHIP

"The growth and development of people is the highest calling...."

— Harvey Samuel Firestone,
Founder of Firestone Tire and Rubber Company and Edison's Travel Companion

Can you think of the first friend you connected with? Why did you connect with them? Was it circumstantial? Did you share some of the same interests? These questions might take you back to your youth, maybe when you were between three to eight years old. Maybe you were in daycare or preschool. Some people do not remember much of their childhood. If this is you, you might be thinking back to between eight and eleven years old. Whenever you connected with your first friend, they played a significant role in your life at that time.

You began to learn how to connect with another person around your age. You learned how to play nice, how to get along with others, and how to build connection. Through everyday interactions with this person, you began the journey of friendship connections. Friendships are one of the most important relationships you can have. Friendships and family relationships make a significant difference in the choices you make, events you go through, celebrations you participate in, and your overall happiness.

Friendships often create the door for new opportunities, such as experiences, travel, and connections. They can even lead to family connections, such as leading you to the person you marry or partner with. Friendships play such a vital role in so many elements of life. They are something to invest in always.

The very first friend I remember really connecting with was a girl in grade school. Our mothers worked together so we became close friends. Through our parents' friendship and their connection as single moms, we ended up living together for several years while they raised us. We grew up like sisters. This experience was wonderful! It was like having an extended support system, and I viewed it as more love in our lives.

As you think back to your first set of friends, maybe you have stayed in contact or maybe, like my connection, you might have lost touch. One thing remains true—these early healthy connections you form will always have a special place in your heart. Hopefully, you can look back at these connections with a warm heart and a smile. Either way, the experiences you had early on started to build a foundation for your connections later.

Experience leads to wisdom. Whether your early experience with friendships was good or bad, you gained wisdom about how you wanted to move forward in connecting with friends. This remains true today. Your experiences with friendships up to this very day will continue to lead you and guide your decisions about whom you want to invest in, how you want to be treated, and how you want to treat others.

Isn't it interesting that we learn from the way we are treated *and* how we treat others? We learn by noting the outcome of our actions with others. Think about this for a minute. The feedback you get from another about actions you take informs how you want to behave and treat others in the future. For example, if you did something to cause another pain, you probably observed anger or sadness in them. If you are perceptive, this non-verbal cue would tell you there might be a situation you need to rectify with this person, this friend. It would also teach you not to do whatever you did again in the future.

Friendships are so important because they continuously teach you how to become a better person, and in return, offer you the rewards of connection and support. For some people, who do not feel connected to their biological family, friendships can take on the particularly key place of family. Connection is all around. Everyone needs a place they feel accepted. Some people find this in their sacred friendships.

EXPLORING NEW FRIENDSHIPS

When clients attend counseling with the goal of creating new and deeper connections with people around them, I begin by asking about their experience with past friendships. I would like you to do the same right now. Grab your journal, paper, or something else to journal your thoughts and go through the following instructions as a self-reflection exercise. Think back to the first time you connected with a friend and ask yourself:

1. What was that experience like?
2. Was it positive or negative and why?

3. What did I learn about the person?
4. What did I learn about myself?

After answering the questions, go on to journal about what you learned and kept with you as you continued to deepen that friendship, or as you chose to move on in search of other connections.

Often, whether the experience was positive or negative, you will find yourself thinking through the events and gaining wisdom to take into your next interaction. These takeaways will help inform future experiences and help you decide which you would like to have and which you want to avoid. With anything in life, self-reflection is a huge asset because it allows you to evaluate experiences, learn from them, grow, and take that wisdom into the future to help you make decisions that will have a positive effect on you and others.

Once you have finished the exercise, it is time to figure out where to find new friendships. Friendship and connection can be found anywhere, but your chance of success lies in finding people with shared interests. If you are looking to find new friends, maybe because you recently went through a life transition, moved, or want to connect with new people, the best places to look are in the activities you enjoy. To begin, think about the things you like to do. What hobbies are you interested in? How do you like to spend your free time? What stage of life are you in? Knowing more about yourself will help you understand more about the friendships you want to form.

Once you have a good understanding of the kind of person you would connect with best, check social media. Are there local groups based on the things you enjoy that meet regularly? For instance, if you have a child in preschool, are there parent groups that meet up? If you are a single adult, is there a singles group? If you love to read books, can you find a local book club? Connecting through your interests will help you find people who are interested in what you are interested in, people who share your hobbies and interests.

Other resources include local community centers and local sports clubs. Even your library may have get-togethers! As you think about which avenue to choose, you may feel a bit of anxiety. Going out on your own may bring up some emotions—that is normal. If you are already connected to someone, bring them with you. If you want to make new connections on your own, challenge yourself to move outside of your comfort zone and show up for something new. The best advice about creating new connections is to take a chance and go for it.

Please understand that your sense of self-protection must be in place in every new adventure. As you explore new friendships, keep your awareness up. When using apps and/or meeting people in person, remember not everyone is good. Be safe. Consider where you are meeting people, what safety measures are in place, and what precautions you want to take. As you get to know new people and understand who they are, you can then relax a little and redefine your boundaries, but never assume you are safe in the beginning.

THE FRIENDSHIP PYRAMID

Now that you have identified some ways to make new connections and create new friendships, it's time to invest. Investing in new and current friendships is much like investing in a romantic relationship, without some of the more intimate aspects. Investing in new friendships is important, but maintaining the investment you put into your current friendships is also important. You do not want a revolving door of friendships that never go beyond the surface. So, make the effort to maintain current friendships while investing in the new ones you are searching for. The exception is if you are trying to get away from an unhealthy friendship. In that case, you would, of course, redefine the boundaries with the current friendship and go on to invest in the new ones you are pursuing.

Surface and in-depth relationships are very different in how they are set up, how they are experienced, and how you invest in them. You, like most, have a variety of friendships at various levels, from surface interactions to in-depth friendships. Imagine a pyramid with the foundation being the widest piece and tapering up to the tip. Surface friendships make up the lowest and widest level of the pyramid—meaning most of the people you interact with daily fall into the surface friendship category. These are the people you have polite conversations with as you pass them in the hall, maybe asking how their family is doing. They are also called acquaintances.

The next level of the friendship pyramid consists of friends who are more than acquaintances, but not people you tell your deepest, darkest secrets to. These are the people you spend some time with. You might enjoy going to dinner or participating in other activities with them; you may even see them every day. They know more about you, and you about them, than your acquaintances do, and you have some deeper, in-depth conversations and connections with them. This level of your pyramid will include the second largest group of people you interact with.

The top level of the pyramid has the fewest people. This is your sacred place where you keep your life protectors. These are people who know you inside and out. You have built two-way trust with them. These are the 2 a.m. people. The people you can call in the middle of the night who will jump out of bed to come help you with whatever you are going through because they are your closest friends. They have seen you at your worst, encouraged you through your best, and always have your back.

Invest time and effort in all three levels of the pyramid. Invest based on your thoughts about whom you will connect with and also whom you can best support. The best friendships and connections go both ways. Don't look only for your best fit, but also look for someone you want to support. To have a good friendship, support must go both ways.

INVESTMENT IN THE FRIENDSHIP

Now that you can identify where people land on your friendship pyramid, how do you invest in them? Investing in friendships involves effort, time, and openness. Once someone who makes you happy is in your life and you make them happy, start deepening the friendship. You do this by showing care and awareness.

Three primary ways exist that you can be there for your friends to help support, grow, and deepen your connection with them. The first is to be there in celebration. When your friend has something exciting happen, you are there to witness and participate in their celebration without requesting anything in return. Second, you can be there when they struggle. When they are struggling, when life has thrown them a curve ball, you can be there to hold their hand and offer gentle and sometimes quiet support. Third, you can be there in their everyday life. When the day calls for jammies, a movie, and pizza, you are there. Having a variety of ways to experience and invest in your friendships is important to growing real, genuine, and authentic connections.

Investing in friendship can mean being available when something happens in your friend's life that is difficult for them to deal with. Events such as car accidents, the death of a loved one, or struggles with their children are all areas where you can step up and show support. Support never has to be offering financial assistance. One of my favorite ways to show support is to send a bag of Hugs in the mail. Hugs are Hershey's Kisses but made with white chocolate striped with milk chocolate. I got this idea from my stepdad. His work assistant had sent him a bag of Hugs years ago when his dog passed away. I saw the effect it had on him and stuck that idea in my pocket. Doing little things for your friends to show them you are there when they are struggling makes a big difference.

Another example of how I have supported a struggling friend was answering the phone, listening, and then inviting them to my house. When this friend arrived, I had a warm bath set for them with a bath bomb and a fresh towel. I invited them to stay as long as they needed, and I said I was there if they wanted to talk. Creating a safe place for your friend helps to deepen the connection and shows them you are solid and will be there for them when they need someone.

Being there to help them celebrate is just as important as being there when things go badly for them. Dale Carnegie's *How to Win Friends and Influence People* is one of the best books I have seen about this topic. The book teaches the reader how important it is to do things like remember people's birthdays. Simply sending a text on a person's birthday shows them you are thinking about them on their special day. It shows them they are in your thoughts, and they are important enough for you to remember them. If you want to go ever further, send an actual card in the mail!

The effort you put into supporting your friends in celebration is just as important as the other efforts you put into the friendship. If they have a wedding, show up. If you cannot show up, send a present or a card. Make the effort to support them in their celebration just as you would like them to do if you achieved a milestone. Reciprocity is vital to the health of friendships.

Finally, pizza and movie night metaphorically means being there to invest in your friends in their everyday life. Do not just invest when they are struggling or celebrating. Invest in the mundane. Granted, adult life is busy. I'm not saying you have to spend time every day investing in your friendships, but you do need to invest in your friends' everyday lives. Occasionally send them a text asking how they are doing. Ask them to coffee or lunch just to catch up. Do things; make contact for no reason other than you were thinking of them and you wanted them to know.

Here's a final note on investing in the friendships you want to grow. To invest and continue to build the friendship, you must be willing to put yourself out there. Take a chance and tell a friend something about you that is genuine and makes you feel a little vulnerable. It could be something you struggle with, dream about, or are passionate about. Test the waters to see how they handle the information. The way they treat the things you share that make you feel a little exposed and vulnerable will tell you if they can be trusted with even deeper, more genuine aspects of your life. This is how you build the top level of your pyramid. Only a couple of people will get the honor of sitting at the top of your pyramid. They are the people you have built trust with and you know will keep your trust. They will become your heart protectors. They will tell you when something seems off and support you through your biggest struggles.

I have a couple of people I consider to be at this top level, and I could not do life without them. They are the people I know I can have fun with but who would also drop everything in a second if I was struggling. Without these people, my life would not be what it is, and I would not feel as strong as I do. Find these people in your life. If you do not have them, start building connections so you can build this part of your pyramid. It takes time, but time will pass whether you invest in your friends or not, so let time pass as you work to strengthen the top section of your pyramid.

LETTING GO OF UNHEALTHY FRIENDSHIPS

It is up to you to choose who you want to keep in your life and call a friend. If a friend is not investing in you, are they someone you want in your life? Just like you should be investing in the people you want as friends, you should look for people who will invest in you. If the investment is not going both ways, you risk being someone's positive supply. Being there to encourage someone is great if you are also receiving encouragement from them. That doesn't mean every act needs to be reciprocated, but support should ebb and flow between you. If you are always giving and never receiving, think about this friendship and ask yourself if you want it to continue.

Of course, leadership roles are different. As the leader, you are meant to provide encouragement and support without expecting it to be reciprocated equally. Leadership roles include being a parent, boss, or mentor. In these roles, you supply encouragement without expecting as much as you give, yet these are still healthy relationships.

Think of a friendship you've had for more than a year. In the last twelve months, did you get or give the majority of the support, or do you believe it was about equal? This is a great question to ask to ensure you are investing and being invested in and the friendship is healthy. If you feel it is lopsided, see if you can create a more balanced friendship. Healthy friendships go both ways.

SUMMARY

Life isn't really healthy without friends. This is a bold, yet true statement. True friendship provides support, encouragement, love, and an environment where trust and authenticity can grow. From belly laughs to crocodile tears, from celebration to grief, friendship plays a valuable role in a happy, healthy life. Your most sacred moments often involve those you honor with the title "friend." Choose wisely, and invest intentionally in those people. You will find so much support to give and experience if you are willing to put the time, effort, love, and space into this essential element of life. Having the pleasure of being part of a true friendship is one of the best experiences you can have on life's journey.

Chapter 19

THE LIGHT OF LIFE EVENTS

"If someday they say of me that in my work, I have contributed something to the welfare and happiness of my fellow man, I shall be satisfied."

— George Westinghouse,
Developed Alternating Current for Light and Power

The moment you take your first breath, you begin to experience your life journey. The undeniable truth is the journey of life brings with it events of all shapes, sizes, and colors. Some of these events are amazing and others are amazingly difficult. And all the events include transitions and decisions you must make. Light is to be found in each event, even those that would smash your light bulb to pieces. That is the beauty within the light bulb effect. Beauty and love can be found everywhere, and in carrying this hope, you can find even more light.

Life events and transitions bring with them a rainbow of emotions and things you must do to get through that chapter of your life. The relationships, friendships, and all you have read to this point will help you uncover the strength you need to get through whatever life brings your way. You may feel alone at times, but continue to reach out and you will find the light. The light does not want to stay hidden. It wants you to find it. Strength does not want to elude you; it wants you to have it.

Situations may make you feel you are not good enough. People may discourage instead of encourage you. The world is full of things that might bring you down, but when you shine your light, you'll see there are also so many things that can bring you up.

Life events, especially the unexpected, are difficult. People tend to thrive on the expected, on routine, on security. Knowing where you will sleep, how you will eat, and that you can pay your bills, increases satisfaction. But finding happiness includes so much more. Friendships, connection, and experiences can all help you find "happy." And they can help you find the light.

You may be thinking about past struggles right now. Maybe you are currently struggling, wondering when the light will come your way. Carry hope and hold it close to your heart. If this feels challenging, open up to someone you trust and ask them to carry the hope for you until you can carry it for yourself. Hope is there for you, even if the struggle is making you think only darkness is waiting. The light is there, waiting, and it wants you to know and experience it.

EXPECTED EVENTS

Light can be found anywhere and is most easily found in joyous celebrations. These events can include a wedding, graduation, new baby, a birthday, or the holidays. Of course, even with joyful events you still may feel some stress and anxiety. While working in the counseling center, a coworker and I used to joke about the holidays. We loved them, but we also loved the quiet after the holiday was over. Typically, one person in the house tends to take the lead in doing the things that make the special event special. That person plans the meals, puts up the decorations, and takes charge. If this is your role, you may notice some extra stress along with the anticipation. You are not alone.

If you are the designated planner, I encourage you to plan the event as you normally do, but then plan an additional day at the end of the holiday or celebration to rest. Pick either the day after the event or a day within the next couple of days. This is your day. Plan to take the day off and do something that recharges your light. In years past, I have planned things like "stay at home spa days," a movie and dinner night, or a night out with friends—something that had nothing to do with the holiday or special event. As you give to others, to ensure your light is fully charged, you must also give to yourself, and you can sometimes do this by planning a self-care day.

Keeping your light charged and shining brightly through special events is the key to continually experiencing the joy that comes with the exciting day. Think about the parts of the event that bring you joy and happiness. If you are an introvert, you may need to plan moments alone; if you are an extrovert, you may need to plan to interact with those attending who help you recharge. Planning a special event does not mean you should stop thinking about your own energy level and what you need to do to take care of yourself through the event.

Keep doing the things you have been learning and practicing. Maintain intentionality to ensure you have the energy to enjoy the event. When you start to feel your light dimming, step away, take some time, and recharge—even if just for a couple of moments. Finally, with every special event, remember to feed your light, along with your body and mind. Make sure you eat throughout the day and drink enough water to stay hydrated. Sometimes events can cause you to forget about taking care of yourself, especially if you are taking care of others. Make each special event joyful by also caring for yourself.

UNEXPECTED EVENTS

Unexpected events are a bit more difficult to engage in fully energized, because by their nature, you are unprepared for them. When an unexpected event comes your way, such as a loss, death, job change, or any other transition, stress rises quickly. The key to maintaining stability is understanding your energy level will drop because it takes energy to engage in unexpected situations. Reaching out to your support group when you feel you may become depleted can help.

Many people facing unexpected events tend to stop taking care of themselves and stop making healthy choices. This lets them focus on what needs to be done at the time, but it's not a sustainable approach. Do what you need to do in the moment, but be careful not to let those moments of necessity become habit. That is the big warning.

Unexpected events can be either welcome or unwelcome. They can bring an array of emotions and actions you must engage in to get through this new journey. It is normal to feel positive and uncomfortable emotions in the midst of these events, and it is also normal to feel these emotions even when the event is something you wanted.

Remember, it is important to normalize the anxiety and sadness that can accompany a desired event. When uncomfortable emotions come up during a desired, yet unexpected event, it can be confusing, but it is all part of any transition. It can be counterintuitive and difficult to understand that even desired events can bring on undesired emotions—as a mental health counselor, I can tell you this is okay and very normal.

FUNCTIONAL AREAS

Functional areas include personal hygiene, grooming, dressing, toileting, eating, sleeping, and functional mobility. In addition to those, I would add two more. The first being your ability to take care of others, such as family, children, and pets. The second would be the ability to provide financial stability to ensure you can afford necessities.

As a therapist, when I help people through an unexpected event, I observe and consider their functional areas. It is important to know your functional areas and how you operate within them. This is called your baseline or your level of homeostasis. Knowing your baseline will help you see when you are outside of your normal, day-to-day functioning. When you understand how you normally engage with the world, you will know when you are *not* engaging normally. You will know something within your system is off, and that can help you make better and healthier decision as you go through unexpected events.

You can investigate other functional areas, also known as activities of daily living (ADL), online.

I tend to focus on the basics when working with clients:

- **Personal hygiene:** Are you brushing your teeth, bathing, brushing your hair, and taking care of the outside of your body?

- **Grooming/dressing:** Has the effort you put into getting ready each day changed? What is your normal when life is going smoothly? Can you put clothing on the correct body parts in the order they should be put on?

- **Toileting:** Are you going to the bathroom regularly? Are you able to clean yourself properly and effectively after using the bathroom? Are you experiencing digestive concerns that may be affecting this area?

- **Eating:** Do you eat regularly scheduled meals that contain nutritious and balanced foods? Have your eating habits changed? The drastic increase or decrease in calorie intake can be a warning that this part of your functional system might be off, so it is worth taking a closer look at what changed.

- **Sleep:** I consider this the key to my daily success. If my sleep is off, everything else gets off. Questions to consider in this area include how much sleep do you need to function at a healthy and productive level? Have you seen a drastic increase or decrease in your ability to fall asleep and/or your ability to stay asleep? Changes in stress levels can significantly affect this functional area.

- **Functional mobility:** Can you move around freely within and outside your home?

With unexpected life events, if these functional areas or ADLs are being affected, you will want to do some self-reflection to understand what is happening in your mind and body to cause the changes. If you can adjust on your own and get yourself back on the road to health and stability, that is fantastic, but my professional advice is don't be afraid to reach out for help, sometimes even to your medical doctor. This is why I have dedicated a whole chapter to this subject—everyone goes through transitions. Sometimes they can find their own way; other times, it's better to reach out for help.

SUMMARY

Thinking back to the expected and unexpected events you have experienced, what helped you move through those changes? What strengths did you recognize? Who were you able to lean on? What did you learn about yourself and the world around you? Take those truths into your future because you will continue to experience life events and transitions as you engage with the world. Remember your functional areas, the activities of daily living. Observe how you interact with these areas when life is running smoothly so you can more easily identify when one or more areas are not working properly and life is not going smoothly. That is when you are at greatest risk of decreased functionality. When you are struggling, if you can be proactive and work on the areas in which you are below your baseline, you will become more resilient.

Also give yourself grace and space to be imperfect. Sometimes during a transition you will be unable to invest in all your functional areas. When this happens, allow yourself space to struggle. Struggling temporarily is okay, but continuing to struggle puts you at risk of getting stuck. Allow yourself to struggle, but do not allow yourself to get stuck there. Remember to reach out for help when you feel the need, when the struggle seems like too much to carry on your own. You now have a new tool in your pocket—the knowledge of your functional areas. This will be like a thermometer for taking your temperature to understand if you are getting sick. When your functional areas are working well, so are you. When you notice you are struggling in any functional area, you know something may be off and it is time to take a closer look at your well-being. Keep taking loving care of yourself and your functional areas and those efforts will reward you. The investment you make in yourself is just as important as the investment you make in others. You deserve what you give to everyone else.

Chapter 20

THE DIM LIGHT OF GRIEF

"I see a friend hurt, and it hurts me, too…."

— Nikola Tesla,
Electrical Engineer and Inventor

No one gets through life without experiencing loss. It is part of the human condition and part of everyone's journey. Grief is multidimensional. The grief you experience each time you lose something or someone will touch several distinct parts of your life. Grief comes with many life events, expected and unexpected, as we discussed in the previous chapter. But you will also experience grief caused by death, which is what we will focus on in this chapter.

Grief affects everyone differently, and your psyche considers several factors when you encounter grief. Processing what feels like darkness is a natural part of the grief journey. If you google the grief cycle, you will find multiple answers that look like the steps to grieving. The thing about grief is it is not a sequential process. You can experience the first element of grief, then the second and third, and then, for no reason whatsoever, jump right back to the first.

Mental health counselors have come to understand the grieving process is not a sequential line going through the stages one by one. Rather, grieving is a process in which everyone finds themselves jumping around to the different elements of grief at random—even when a jump is most unexpected. These unexpected jumps in the grief process can bring additional emotions to the surface, which can be confusing.

Confusion is the emotional cousin to grief. It sits in the background, pushing your mind to question reality. This may seem concerning, but it is good for the healing process. Confusion is uncomfortable for the grieving person, but it has a distinct and important purpose in the process. Confusion, much of the time, arises to help your brain ask questions and spur healing and understanding. When working with clients, I encourage them to question the confusion as if it is a person trying to tell them something. I tell them confusion is a healthy part of the process and life's journey. So, as we get deeper into the grief process, know that confusion is part of the mix like everything else, and it is a normal part of the grieving process.

THE GRIEF PROCESS

Pretty much everyone experiences the same elements in the grieving process, though they may experience them in a different order. The most common elements when someone loses a loved one include denial, anger, bargaining, depression, and acceptance. Some people think these are stages. Once you go through denial, you move to anger. Once you go through anger, you move to bargaining, and so on until you reach acceptance. I challenge this belief and present a more chaotic, but also more grace-filled approach to the way we look at the grief cycle.

People who are grieving may first go through denial, but they may not. They may feel angry from the beginning and then skip to depression and then back to denial and so on. The way the brain processes grief depends on so many variables there really is no one fit for all.

I say all this to provide comfort—there is no right or wrong way to grieve. If you are thinking about a loved one you lost right now and how you grieved, it was most likely the right way for you to process grief. Do not compare your grief to that of others because their journey may require them to experience the loss differently.

DIFFERENT KINDS OF LOSSES

Grief comes from both expected and unexpected losses. The first time I experienced loss outside the natural course of life (I lost a grandparent when I was in sixth grade) was the suicide of a friend in high school. I was at a friend's house when my friend said he had something to tell me. I knew it was serious by the way he looked. I sat down beside him, and he told me our friend had taken his life. Mostly in disbelief, I excused myself to go to the bathroom. I looked into the mirror, trying to make sense of the emotions I was feeling. I immediately landed in denial and confusion. The loss was difficult to process, but the support in our friendship group helped everyone who knew him. This grief was unexpected.

Other unexpected losses include unforeseen medical conditions, accidents, and homicide. Any unexpected loss brings unusual circumstances that loved ones must face in addition to the regular grieving process. When an unexpected loss occurs, the surviving loved ones may have questions, be confused, and have difficulty processing thoughts they had not encountered before the event. That is because you cannot prepare for unexpected grief. Grief comes as an unwanted and unwelcomed surprise. It means doing all the thought work after the loss, rather than having time to prepare yourself like you can when you know someone is ill and about to die.

People who experience unexpected grief may also struggle with regret. Regrets about things they wanted to say, but never had the chance or the courage to say. They can regret the missed opportunities to share experiences with the person who is no longer here. With unexpected grief, there is no time to grieve before the event, and this can make it difficult to feel closure after the fact.

Complicated grief can play a big part in unexpected grief. Complicated grief occurs when the loss is not typical and is unrelated to natural causes. In March 2022, this kind of grief was added to the DSM-5 TR, *The Diagnostic and Statistical Manual of Mental Health Disorders.* This is the book used by mental health counselors to diagnose mental disorders.

An example of expected grief and loss could be when a loved one has been battling cancer for some time and passes away. Another example could be when a person dies from complications related to old age or has been dealing with a known medical condition for an extended period of time. The people left behind often have time to say goodbye to their loved one because with expected grief, time together can be embraced as part of the grieving journey. This may not make the loss any easier, but it may leave fewer regrets than with a sudden loss. If you know of someone who is, or you yourself are, facing a known medical condition, embrace the time you have left. Think about the way you want to spend this precious time given to you. Say the things you want to say; do the things you can do. You will find yourself going through a grieving journey, but you have some time to make your heart's desires known to the people closest to you.

Finally, we have delayed grief. Delayed grief is when you don't know about the loss until several weeks or even months later, or you learn a loved one you have not seen in years has passed. With this kind of grief, you still go through the various "stages" of the grieving process, just some time after the event.

SUPPORTING YOURSELF IN GRIEF

When you have been touched by the loss death brings, give yourself grace. This means when you experience a loss, give yourself the things that comfort you. Suspend your weight-loss diet. Spend more time with friends and family. Maybe even take a trip you always said you were going to take. Allow yourself the grace to get a little off track with your plans because loss brings a different journey to your door. Yes, you have responsibilities and reasons why the above advice may not work, but you also need some self-compassion when loss comes along. Of course, do these things within reason so you don't make choices that will lead you down a truly unhealthy path, but when you experience loss, it is not the time to stick to rigid plans. When you experience loss, it is time to take comfort in life and the things that bring you peace as you go through the grieving process.

Things you can do to help you process loss include journaling, reaching out to friends and family, and continuing to take care of yourself. Hold space for your loss like you would for a close friend. Allow yourself to cry, be mad, and question. Allow yourself to feel the emotions. Allow yourself to be confused. When you are struggling, tell yourself, "It is okay to struggle." Allowing yourself to see all the emotions you are feeling, the thoughts you are having, and the struggles you are carrying reflects the important role the person you are grieving for played in your life.

Word of caution: If you are currently experiencing grief and have lost all interest in your normal daily functional areas such as friends, family, taking care of yourself, and the other ADLs listed in the previous chapter, or if you are having thoughts of self-harm or suicide, please call the National Suicide Hotline at: 988.

DELIVERY AND TIMING

If you know someone going through the grieving process, or who is about to, you can offer support in several ways. First, let's look at having to tell someone that a person they care for has passed. This is both a heart-wrenching and honored position—honored because you are in the sacred place of being able to create a supportive and loving environment for the bereaved when you communicate the sad news. Take this moment seriously and pack it with love.

When the person has already passed and there is nothing more to do, it is a lot different than when timing is critical and you only have a short time to communicate to those who need to know about the loss. The first thing to do is to ask yourself if the news is urgent or do you have time to put some love and thought into how you can compassionately communicate the loss.

When put in the position of having to tell someone a loved one has passed, consider timing. Recently, a friend called to ask for advice. She wanted to know if it was okay to wait to tell a friend (because she was on vacation) that her friend had died. I asked how close they were, and my friend said they were not close anymore. I advised her to wait until the friend came home from vacation.

Another example is when you have to give the bad news that someone has passed to a parent with young children. In this case, it may be a good idea, if timing allows, to text them to see if they have time to talk before calling them. This gives them time to get their children settled and lets them know you need their full attention.

You may find yourself with some time to communicate the loss, such as a parent telling a child a grandparent has passed. My grandmother passed while I was on a trip with my stepdad. He waited until the end of the trip when we were on our way home to tell me. He pulled over and asked if I wanted to take a walk on the beach before we headed home. I got out of the car, and gently, while walking on the beach, he told me about my grandma. Delivery and timing are both important when informing someone about a death.

ACTS OF KINDNESS

With the death of a loved one, thinking starts to run slowly and life tasks tend to get ignored. We can always offer support to someone who has experienced loss in the tried-and-true ways such as offering food, cleaning services, watching their children, and so on. It is important to note that when someone is grieving, they may not know what they need. Often, people at funerals will tell the bereaved, "Call me if you need anything." The bereaved will nod, and most likely, never call. The best thing you can do for someone who is grieving is to be proactive. Send a meal, send a card telling them you are thinking of them, send them a loving text. They may not realize what they need in the moment, but by you being proactive, they will feel supported. A mentor from years ago told me they would rather someone know they loved them too much than have them question if they loved them at all. It is better to show support and be in danger of showing too much love than to leave people wondering if you love them. (Of course, sticking to respectful boundaries is important when taking this approach.)

RANDOM REMEMBRANCES

One of the best ways to show support I use with those I love is to show support several months after the loss. Right after the funeral, the person will have a lot of support because the loss is fresh in people's minds, but six months after the funeral, most people will have gone back to their everyday lives—except the person who experienced the grief. They will continue to live with a hole in their heart, someone missing at Christmas, someone not there to chat or make memories with, to get support from and to give support to.

An easy way to support those around you who experience loss is to do something for them several months or even a year later. (Set a reminder on your calendar.) For example, on the one-year anniversary, send them an unexpected card in the mail, take them out to lunch, or drop off their favorite coffee. Ongoing support is just as important as immediate support. Showing your loved one you remember their loss will have a positive effect on their grief cycle and show them they are still not alone in carrying the loss. It honors the one who passed and the ones they left behind.

The best quote I have come across about loss and those left behind was when Keanu Reeves was being interviewed by Stephen Colbert. Colbert asked Reeves what he thinks happens when we die, to which Reeves responded, "The ones we leave behind miss us tremendously."

When given the honor of supporting another as they grieve, handle them with loving care, compassion, and patience. They are going through one of the grimmest times anyone can experience. Show grace for the array of emotions they may be feeling and the things they may say. It is possible grief will make them say things they do not really mean. Understand they are probably trying to survive. Have grace and hold space for them so they can find their healing. Be their support without asking for anything in return.

WHAT NOT TO DO

Knowing what *not* to do when someone experiences a loss is as important as knowing what to do. So many clients have come into my office with horror stories about the things people have said to them or done for them that were supposedly supportive but had just the opposite effect.

Grief needs space and time to heal. This may mean sitting silently by your loved one, saying nothing. Just being there for another person in their pain can provide worlds of support.

Many want to take action to lessen their loved one's pain. This causes people to say and do things that do not have the intended effect. In grief, quiet support is one of the best approaches. You cannot take the pain away for your loved one; grief is a process they must go through, and it includes feeling the pain.

Avoid offering too much advice, such as telling them to take comfort in those they still have, trying to offer solutions to "fix" their grief, and for sure, do not try to "one-up" their grief. Your loved one does not need to know you have experienced something worse, even if you have. Your loved one just needs you to be there for them, without imposing your own past hurts. Being fully present for your loved one in that moment is one of the best things you can do for them.

SUMMARY

Grieving or supporting someone who is grieving is a difficult road filled with a variety of emotions that need space to be processed. Losing a loved one, no matter the situation, can leave a hole in the hearts of those who knew them. When anyone dies, the world changes, and we must adjust. As you think back on times you experienced grief through loss, offer yourself space, love, and patience for healing. This is a journey, not something you can rush. Allow yourself time to experience healing; you will not forget, but the pain of the loss will lessen. Do not hold onto the anger out of fear of forgetting your loved one. You can let the anger go. Your love for that person will remain.

Section 6

SUSTAINING THE FUTURE

"Everybody in the world is seeking happiness—and there is one sure way to find it. That is by controlling your thoughts. Happiness doesn't depend on outward conditions. It depends on inner conditions."

— Dale Carnegie,
How to Win Friends and Influence People

Chapter 21

THE LIGHT OF CAREER

"Our greatest weakness lies in giving up. The most certain way to success is always to try just one more time."

— Thomas Edison,
American Scientist

Every person experiences their own unique journey to adulthood, making their own decisions and coming to their own forks in the road at various times. The decisions you make about your career will affect everything from how much time you have to spend with your family to how much freedom you get to experience. If you make proactive choices during this important developmental stage, you may also prevent yourself from having to struggle financially later. Something I learned early on was freedom and finances are closely related. Your career path will inform those two elements of your life, which will set the foundation for your adulthood.

One day when I was younger, I was sitting in the car thinking about what I wanted to be when I grew up and about my relationship with money. I realized that even having a little money opened up freedom to make choices. I did not feel the need to be wealthy, but I wanted enough funds to experience making choices confidently. I did not need to have it all; I just wanted to have some. As I grew up, I was lucky enough to have a mentor who introduced me to the idea of going to college. I was excited to fill out my first college application, not even knowing what I was doing!

Being willing to walk through the door of opportunity is all you need to do to keep pursuing your goals, and that is true for your career as well. You might not know where you'll end up, but if you stay involved and engaged in life, doors will open. The first step for me was going to college, something I didn't think I would do. For others, that first step might be going to trade school, going to work right after high school, or obtaining your GED. I encourage you, at minimum, to get your GED. Any of those accomplishments will open doors if you stay engaged and don't stop trying. Do not give up.

PURSUING YOUR PROFESSIONAL BEST

One person's professional best might look very different from another person's. Begin by finding your passions and how you like to engage in life. What are your personal and professional goals, and what will it take to achieve them? Do you believe you can do it? If not, do not let that stop you. Continue going toward that goal until the door closes absolutely. Even then, there might be a back door you could take to reach your goal. How badly do you want it? Will you quit when someone tells you no, or will you take that rejection and use it to feed your passion to continue?

Your answers to the questions above will help you discover and pursue your professional best. Do not sell yourself short. If you think you can run that extra mile, professionally speaking, do it. Let your light shine and believe you can do it. If you have a goal and you have seen someone accomplish it, then you know it is possible. If you work hard enough, you can get there as well. With enough work, enough dedication, and enough effort, what you desire is within reach. You can get to the place you have always dreamed of getting to.

Reflect on the things that dim your light professionally. Is it a loved one not believing in you? Is it not having the education you need? Maybe it is a lack of supplies? Think about what others did to gain those things. Could you hire a mentor to guide you to achieve your goals? Could you go to school to learn the knowledge needed? Could you work a second job to save for the supplies you need to pursue your true professional passion? You have it within you to accomplish bigger things than you ever imagined—you just have to start.

WHEN TO SHINE BRIGHTLY

Your career begins with your resume. That is where you need to shine. Invest time, energy, and research into putting together the best resume you can. It needs to look professional. Make sure it is typed and printed with your name and contact information at the top. Add your objective and work history starting with your most recent position, going backwards chronologically down the page to your oldest position within the last ten years. For each position, list the company's name, the month and year you began working there, and the month and year you stopped working there. Include your job responsibilities and accomplishments at each job. Include details about your education, skills, and other experiences.

When you interview for a new position, if you show up any less than ten minutes early, you are late. Show up early! This makes a great impression on the person you will meet. They will notice when you arrived. Interviews are your time to shine. Do not be afraid to sound confident in discussing your qualifications, what you bring to the table, and your experiences.

One of my favorite (and very cliché) questions to ask people I interview is "What are your strengths and weaknesses?" I honestly do not really care what the answer is since everyone has strengths and weaknesses. What I look for is how honest and genuine the individual is in their response. Continue to shine your light brightly when going in for an interview. Let the interviewer see your best! Be genuine and authentic. Prepare questions beforehand so you can learn more about the potential job and appear interested. After all, it must be a good fit both ways.

Call your potential employer two days after the interview to thank them for their time and ask if you can provide any other information. Finally, send them a handwritten card thanking them for the time they spent with you during the interview. Shining brightly on the path to the career you want will mean putting yourself out there to make sure you get noticed. You want to put your best foot forward, and showing the company you are highly interested increases your odds of landing that position.

WHEN TO DIM YOUR LIGHT

Once you have successfully landed the position you want, it is time to get to work. Make sure you understand what the company expects of you. The best way to do that is to read the company policies and your employee contract. Each company has drastically different expectations, and these documents will not be the same from one company to another. Understanding policy can help your light shine in a beautiful way. During the interview process, you wanted your light to shine brightly. You wanted to be noticed. Now that you have the position, you want your light to keep shining. You are there to support the company, and by doing so, you will find your own success.

If you have landed a position in a company you love and you want to stay there for years, the best way to ensure that is to work your way up the chain of command. You can do this by being proactive in your decisions, in the way you work with those who are in higher management positions, and also by supporting those at the same level as you. Showing your leaderships skills before you become a leader helps you get noticed by those who are currently leading.

Once you get to a leadership position, this is where you want your light to become humble. Leaders are actually the servants of those they lead. In my position as the owner and clinical director, I tell my staff as their leader it is my job to work for them. It is my responsibility to make sure they have the supplies they need to do their job (the job I hired them to do). It is my job to make sure they have the training they need. It is my job to support them however I can and help them do the best job they can. If they fail, I evaluate what I could have done better as a leader. The higher you go up the chain of command, the softer you want your light to be so the light of those you lead can shine brightly.

THE LIGHT OF MENTORSHIP

If you are established in your career and have gained wisdom about what does and doesn't work, consider sharing your light through mentoring. The light of mentoring is an inspirational journey where you share your wisdom with another to help brighten their light. Mentorships can be boss to employee, coworker to coworker, or contractor to client—where someone hires you to help lead their path. The light of mentorship is so important to participate in once you get to a place in your career where you feel confident in your skills. You will not only be helping someone else, but you will learn more yourself in the process of mentoring others.

In the counseling world, mentorship comes through internships. A clinical supervisor oversees an intern who is typically still in their graduate program or has recently finished their coursework but is still looking to gain hours toward licensure. Mentorship between an intern and a supervisor tends to include weekly or bi-weekly discussions. The supervisor sets aside thirty to sixty minutes to help guide the new counselor's path.

Outside of the counseling world, mentorships can be beneficial to companies who are looking to grow their staff and would like to deepen the knowledge their current employees have. By allowing time for mentoring and supervision in the work schedule, companies can deepen the quality of the services and products they produce as their staff builds expertise on the end product and how to make it the best it can be. When you invest in your staff, you are investing in your company and the overall quality of your product.

THE LIGHT OF EDUCATION

Whatever industry you are in, always continue to grow. Through sharpening your skill, you will also increase your value as a leader, boss, employee, or intern. The information out there for you to learn is endless. Learn how to sharpen your skills and teach others how to sharpen theirs. Search out ideas on inspiring those around you to do better, and set goals to do better yourself. Books on time management, managing others, increasing your skills, or whatever subject you want to deepen your knowledge in are out there. Maybe you don't think you have time or you have no interest in reading. Then listen to a book during your drive to and from work. Knowledge is insight, and having insight will help you do better at your job.

When you increase your knowledge and your ability to get the job done, you increase your worth. Think of knowledge as an investment in yourself as an employee, a leader, a boss, a mentor, and possibly even an owner. The more you learn, the more confident you will be, which will help you do the things that will make you successful. The more successful you are, the more income you will enjoy. The more income, the more freedom you will have.

Here is both a secret and a word of caution: Do not shoot for making a lot of money and becoming wealthy. Shoot for happiness, job satisfaction, doing the things you love, and making just enough to sustain the kind of lifestyle you want so you can be free. If you only strive for being financially wealthy, you risk becoming a slave to money, and imbalance will seep into your life. Money alone does not create success. Success is created by freedom, happiness, love, and stability. Earning enough to afford the things you need creates freedom, but that freedom will be worthless if you sacrifice everything else in the end.

The goal of education is to increase your worth, but the goal of increasing your worth is not just making money. The goal of increasing your worth is to be free. When you make enough to pay your bills, save, invest, and enjoy life, you will feel free. Happiness is the ultimate goal. Don't let money put you in a metaphorical jail where your freedom is lost because you are more focused on making money than on being happy.

SUMMARY

Though this is not a comprehensive chapter about career development, it provides a great start for thinking about your own career advancement and the "why" behind making money. Hundreds of books related to career development are waiting for you if this is an area you are interested in investigating further. Remember, you want to earn money to experience freedom, but not at the price of your happiness. Also remember that your light will help inspire and brighten other people's lights in the career world. Sometimes it will be your turn to shine brightly; other times, it will be your turn to dim your light so others can shine. In any company, when everyone works together and has an opportunity to shine brightly, the company becomes a wonderful place to work where both the staff and the company can thrive.

Chapter 22

THE LIGHT OF FINANCES

"The first step toward getting somewhere is to decide that you are not going to stay where you are."

— J. P. Morgan,
American Financier and Industrialist

Finances can create a bold sense of freedom, or they can create heavy stress. As we discussed in the previous chapter, if you can build a stable relationship with your finances, it can bring you a lot of freedom. If you have a poor relationship with finances, it can lead to a lot of anxiety, worry, and stress. The way you approach your finances will dictate many of the outcomes in your life. Everything from your credit score to what you eat daily will be influenced by the way you interact with your personal finances.

While living under your parents' roof, you may watch them buy things without really understanding how much a house costs compared to a car, or how much fast food costs compared to a five-star restaurant. As you get older, you start to understand how finances work and that a drive-thru cheeseburger costs a lot less than a sit-down restaurant's juicy gourmet burger. You also begin to realize how those things taste drastically different, and in those metaphorical decisions, you start to develop the way you will interact with money.

Finances and time are closely related. Reflect on how you spend your money. Then think about how you spend your time. These are connected. How you spend one affects how you spend the other. As you continue to read about the light of finances, also reflect on the way you spend time. Both are equally valuable.

EARNING AND DEBT

Before you do anything with finances, you must learn how to earn money. It all begins with getting and keeping a job. Your job could be a nine-to-five position or you could get paid to create. It could involve traveling or office work. You could also choose to become an expert in a trade. The number of things you can create that will equate to a paycheck has no limit. You can get paid for a wide variety of things when you put in the effort. You can also choose to work for someone else or go into business for yourself. How you decide to earn money is the first quest you will engage in on your financial journey.

When should people start working? Everyone's answer is different based on their needs and abilities. Earning money begins with taking a chance and putting yourself out there—sending in resumes, scheduling interviews, and making follow-up calls. Once you have a job (a way of earning stable and reliable income), your focus should turn to ensuring you make responsible decisions, like showing up on time to your job, calling in when you are sick, and doing the best work you can based on the job's responsibilities and expectations. If you do, you should be well on your way to earning a solid living.

Once you have some funds, what should you do with them? Great question! Start by opening a checking account *and* a savings account. The first thing you do when you get each paycheck is pay yourself. That means put at least 5 percent of your money into your savings account and *do not touch it.* Save until you have at least two months' worth of expenses in your savings account. What do you do with that 5 percent you are saving after you have two months of funds in your savings? Open an investment account and start funding an investment goal. Talk to your bank about finding a financial planner who can provide additional advice. Talk to your parents, your friends, and anyone you know whom you can glean information from about how to become financially stable.

Debt—let's talk about it. Most people have some debt. Set a goal to get out of debt, and do *not* continue to build debt. Get a credit card if you feel you will be able to pay it off every month. If not, do not open a credit account until you are confident you can accomplish that goal. If you have a car payment, credit card payment, house payment, or any other kind of debt, write it all down in a one-page document. Include how much you owe, what your monthly payments are, what the interest rates are, and when you expect to have this debt paid off.

Next, organize this list from smallest debt to largest. Every month, put a little extra toward your smallest debt. When the smallest debt is paid off, put the extra toward the next smallest debt on your list. Follow this process until you are out of debt. Challenge yourself to make extra payments every month, because remember, the goal of having a healthy relationship with finances is to experience happiness and freedom. When you are in debt, you are not free in the same way you will be when you are out of debt.

SAVING AND GIVING

When I was in middle school, I got my first job babysitting a neighbor's two kids. At the time, I charged $1.00 per hour. I worked about four hours on the weekend and usually brought home $5.00 after the tip. I thought I was on top of the world until I spoke with my stepdad. He made me put half of everything I earned into my savings account. I was so upset; I could not believe I was bringing home $5.00 and only got to spend $2.50. Back then, that was a lot of money. But I did as he encouraged, and when the time came to purchase my first car, I had $2,000 to put toward it. To this day, I tell my kids they must get into the habit of saving money from an early age because, though it hurts a little at the time, when you need that money, it will be available.

Saving money is one of the most important disciplines you can acquire. No one wants to do it in the beginning, but it almost becomes addictive once you get into the habit of watching your accounts grow. The more you save, the more you have.

Giving is just as important as saving because giving will teach you how to be generous. You must decide for yourself how much you can give. This is the second discipline related to finances I highly encourage you to adopt. When you give, not only do you help another, but you apply and strengthen the kindness and compassion in your heart for the wellbeing of others.

Learning how to manage your money and developing the two disciplines of saving and giving will help your light become brighter and grow not only your finances, but also your connection to other humans through compassion and empathy. If I were to look at someone's check register, even before I spoke with them, I would already know a lot about them just by the way they spend their money. What would you like other people to know about you from the way you spend your money? We all pass through different seasons. Sometimes it is a season to hunker down and save; other times, you find yourself free to be more generous. Know that saving and giving go hand in hand.

EXPANDING YOUR WEALTH

Think about the goals you would like to accomplish in the next five years. In the next ten years. Now think about the funds you will need to support those goals. Do you have the means to accomplish those goals based on your current income? If you do, great! Start saving for those goals. If not, think about how you could increase your income so you could accomplish those goals.

You can expand your wealth through creative thinking, developing plans, and following through. Do not just wait for opportunities to come to you—create them. What step could you take tomorrow that would move you an inch closer to your goals? This chapter is only an introduction to get you started thinking about the financial world around you—there is so much more to know.

The financial world also involves asking yourself how you want to invest, how you want to save, what you want your retirement to look like, and what opportunities might come your way for increasing your income. Various books and approaches for strengthening your relationship with finances are out there. A word of warning about anything that seems too good to be true. Get rich plans often lead to the person behind them getting rich and everyone who follows them spending a lot of money to get nowhere. You only have to look on YouTube to see nightmare stories of people who got involved with multi-level marketing schemes only to find what was promised was not what was delivered.

Going forward, be careful and thoughtful about how you interact with your finances. Read books, watch videos, and observe successful people and their finances. Ask questions! Work hard to learn to balance financial responsibilities, because when you find the balance, you will find a sense of freedom and happiness.

Time and money are often closely related, and learning to save one will also help you learn to save the other. Your brain will start thinking more logically and concisely, in a highly creative way, as you continue to work to save both time and money.

SUMMARY

The light of financial freedom comes from a lot of dedicated work and can be accomplished with time, and follow through. If you are in debt right now, know you do not need to be in debt forever. If you do not know how to save and invest, do the research and learn how to improve your situation. Financial freedom is waiting, and a lot of information on how to attain it is readily accessible on the internet. When you start to feel discouraged, set smaller goals. When you accomplish those goals, your new sense of pride will spur you on to believe you can do even more.

Each achievement, big or small, will give your confidence a boost and help you believe in yourself. If you can accomplish that, you can accomplish the next step. Remember, just because you are more confident does not mean you will not also carry doubt. If you don't let the doubt win, you can keep moving toward your goals. Do not just wait for the opportunity to come to you—create it.

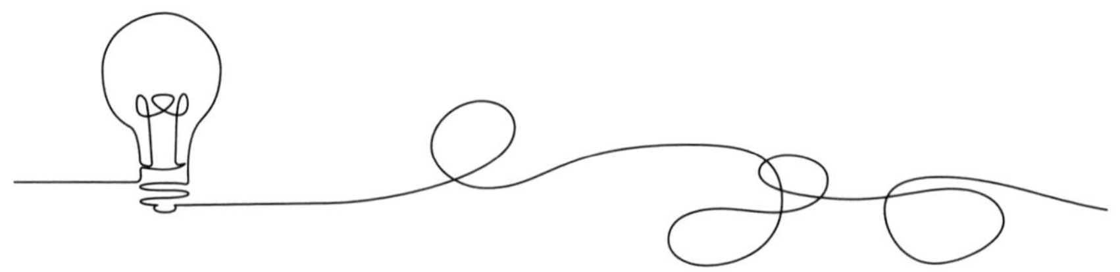

Chapter 23

THE LIGHT OF NEW BEGINNINGS

"There is no substitute for hard work."

— Thomas Edison,
Inventor of the Alkaline Storage Battery

Whew! What a journey this book has been! At this point, you have picked up some good habits to increase the light within and the light you share with others. Hopefully, this book has taught you about the light you hold, how to strengthen others' lights, and how to work through the dim times. Light is all around to be discovered. Sometimes you will be the light for others, and sometimes your light will be dim, and you will need others to share their light with you.

You might find it easy to help others, but more difficult to ask for help. As you continue to grow your light, work on asking for help. When you ask for help, it gives others a chance to serve. Think about that again—when you ask for help, you are providing another person with a chance to share their light with you. In doing so, both your lights become stronger. Do not be afraid to ask for help when you feel your light getting low.

Self-improvement is a journey filled with self-reflection, growth, and internal empowerment. Hopefully, you will find yourself taking chances and trying new things even more. Become comfortable with being more engaged in the world around you. When you are engaged, doors of opportunity will open. You might even find yourself in the curious position of having so many doors open for you that you will have to choose which ones to walk through and which ones to leave behind! Once opportunity starts to find you, your eyes will open to a whole new world of possibilities you may never have realized were waiting for you to explore.

THE LIGHT IN OTHERS

The Light Bulb Effect is not just about growing your own light—it's about helping to grow the light of those around you. When you do this, everyone becomes stronger. When you give of your light, you lose nothing. The act of giving will add to your strength.

The journey is not just about realizing we all have some damage we carry with us, but realizing we are in this together. Healing is stronger when we can be more genuine, authentic, and connected.

Going back to the beginning, when the light bulb broke in my hand as I was decorating for Halloween, I never imagined the journey that moment would take me on or the things I would share with others. All because of that one moment. That moment led me to so many connections and open doors because I was willing to engage in the moment. I left anger on the floor and chose to look at that moment from an unfamiliar perspective. And really, that is all it takes to change your direction—one moment of being open to what the world has to offer. Goodness is waiting for you.

MEANING

The meaning behind *The Light Bulb Effect* is one everyone can relate to and use to grow. Everyone who travels on life's highway will cross paths with hurt. Life has a way of breaking people. But in brokenness, there is so much beauty and healing to experience. You just have to keep trying. You may feel lost right now. You may feel life does not carry the same promise for you as it does for others. I can tell you, I relate and have been in a similar position. The darkness can feel so strong, almost never ending—especially in times when you feel alone in the world, like you have no support. In those times, the darkness is lying to you, and the light is just waiting for an opportunity to penetrate your heart. Remember, in darkness is where light can be found.

Engage in life because the light is waiting, hoping you will find it, and when you do, it holds so much goodness for you. When you are stuck in the darkness, sometimes engaging in life seems overwhelming. During those times, try to move toward the light, even if just an inch closer. If an inch seems too much, as it sometimes can, make it your goal to move just a centimeter. Whatever you do, do not stop growing toward the light. Don't believe the lie that darkness is all that is left for you. The lie feels strong and true, sometimes totally convincing. Ultimately, it is still a lie. The light is waiting for you. Just move a little closer. It wants you to find it.

Find the things that give you strength. Find the things that give you hope. Hold on to those things when life feels dark, and wait for the light to come, because it will come if you do not give up. The only thing the darkness needs to grow is lack of hope. If you can find even a glimmer of something to hope for, of something to hold on to, the light will find you. This might not happen overnight, and in fact, for most people, it will not happen for days, weeks, months, or sometimes years. The chapter of life spent in darkness can feel never-ending, but if you don't give up and continue to search for it, the light will find you.

AUTHENTICITY, VULNERABILITY, GENUINENESS

My three favorite qualities in people are authenticity, vulnerability, and genuineness. I have discovered these three things in others feed my light. Continue to discover what feeds your light, and then search out people who have those qualities. Authenticity, vulnerability, and genuineness help grow the light in the world. Other traits such as kindness, gentleness, compassion, and empathy also carry light with them.

Do you know the areas you carry that help spread light into the world? They are the things the people around you are attracted to in your personality. If you don't know the light you bring to the table, ask your friends and family because they know. They see it. Your light is why they choose to spend time with you.

Everyone carries darkness, but everyone also carries light. These two elements will always struggle, and what you choose to do with them, how you choose to interact with them, will determine which side grows bigger. Though you may not always feel in control of these elements, you can choose which ones to invest in at any given moment. The light never leaves. The darkness tries to stay, but darkness cannot live where there is light. Though the struggle is tough, you are not alone. The light is patiently waiting for you.

SUMMARY

Your new beginning starts now. Actually, your new beginning started the moment you picked up this book and started reading. You are now on a journey to grow, heal, and mend your light. Notice how you shine brighter around others. Stop dimming your light around those who intimidate you. You are worthy and valued. If someone or something is in your life creating darkness, think about what your light needs to continue to shine brightly around that person or situation, and go for it!

A Final Note

TAKING THE LIGHT OF ACTION

"When motivation cannot be found, allow discipline to do the work."
— Jennifer Michelle

Entrepreneur, Published Author, Business Owner

Action time! It is time to start applying what you learned in this book to your everyday life. You invested time and energy into reading this book. The next step is to act on the knowledge you gained. Don't just read this book and set the wisdom aside. Embrace the thoughts you had, the goals you set, and the dreams you imagined. What actions can you take? What action steps are you going to implement? It is time to set some goals. Write them down. Post them where you can see them every day. You *can* make it happen!

Don't let worry and doubt steal your motivation. When you can't find motivation, let discipline do the work. That is the secret to success. Those who only put the work in when motivated will not experience the rewards to be uncovered by working when motivation leaves. You need discipline on your journey. Work when you are motivated, but don't stop there. Also work at your goals when you are not motivated. Use discipline as your guide when you are unable to find motivation.

I challenge you to act. Not in a month or two weeks from now, but tomorrow. This book came to fruition thanks to my business coach. I had been working with him for several months, when during one of our monthly calls, he asked about my book idea. I told him about it and that I had been thinking about writing it for years. He said it was time. I took a big gulp and said okay. He asked how I felt about it, and I told him I did not believe I could do it, but I believed in him and his belief in me. If he believed I could do it, I would believe in his belief. He asked when I could begin. I looked at my calendar and said in about two weeks. He told me that did not work—I needed to start tomorrow. So, I began the process of writing this book the very next day. Do not wait to begin your process. Your time is now.

The new strategies you learned in this book and knowing what to do will not create change. You need to decide it is your time to act and make the change happen. If you read one hundred books on self-help but never implement any of that knowledge in your daily life, you will not be any farther in your journey than you were when you started reading. The light is waiting for you to find it. It is waiting for you to engage. Start engaging. Start growing. Start healing.

ACTIVITY

List ten action items you want to begin to act on to make your light brighter. Write these down and begin working toward accomplishing these new goals. The light is waiting for you to find it. Search for it and figure out what it needs to grow. The time is now. Begin today.

CALL TO ACTION

In this book you learned everyone carries a metaphorical light bulb. Each person's light bulb starts out whole, unbroken, unscarred. Through the journey of life, you realized the light bulb can be fragile at times. In these times, it gets scratches, scars, and sometimes even breaks. *But*—there is so much hope—hope in the journey of healing. And there is beauty in the imperfections. *The Light Bulb Effect* is about finding the wholeness and light within your broken pieces. Glance again at the front cover of this book. The light bulb on the cover is not whole. It is not unbroken; in fact, it is made up of a lot of little pieces of broken glass that make up the whole light bulb. When you realize the beauty of life comes out in your pieces, you will find your wholeness. Wholeness is not found in being perfect; rather, it is found in realizing you are both broken and valuable. This is where you will discover the strength of your light.

If you apply the wisdom you gained in this book, you will begin to find comfort, self-acceptance, and strength as you recognize the light you carry—the light you have always carried. When you apply what you have learned, you can find peace among your pieces.

Now that you have read my book, I encourage you to contact me to tell me what you liked and what you did not like so I can improve it for the next printing. More importantly, tell me about you! I would love to know the challenges you face, what your obstacles are so I can help you. I would also love to offer you a no-obligation, thirty-minute coaching consultation via secure video platform to see how I can help you reach your goals.

Please email me at jennifer@jennifermichellecoaching.com with your time zone, and we will schedule your complimentary consultation.

I truly wish you the best of luck on your journey to healing and strengthening your light.

All the best,

Jennifer Michelle

Jennifer Michelle

ABOUT THE AUTHOR

JENNIFER MICHELLE is an author, professional keynote speaker, Licensed Clinical Professional Counselor (LCPC), professional business coach, and entrepreneur. She has had feature articles in *Thrive Global, UP Journey,* and *Authority Magazine.* Jennifer earned her master's degree in marriage and family counseling from Northwest Nazarene University, specializing primarily in couples therapy using techniques from Emotionally Focused Therapy and the Systems model. She also specializes in trauma counseling using approaches based on Eye Movement Desensitization and Reprocessing (EMDR) therapy.

Jennifer is a Registered Clinical Supervisor in Idaho, and a Nationally Certified Counselor (NCC). As a supervisor, she has successfully helped new counselors and graduate-level interns become licensed in Idaho.

In 2008, Jennifer opened Family Counseling Services, a community mental health agency, in Meridian, Idaho. She has since grown the agency and opened a second location in Boise, Idaho. Jennifer's agency is focused on providing compassionate, ethical care to their clinical and community clients. One quality Jennifer is passionate about and to which she attributes much of her agency's success is focusing on staff cohesion and satisfaction while providing excellent client care. She believes if staff members feel supported and have what they need to do their jobs, the quality of client care and services will be greatly improved, resulting in growth for the client, the staff, and the agency.

Jennifer has led many seminars on topics in the helping professions. She is the author of *The Light Bulb Effect* and the upcoming book *The Finance Diet*.

Jennifer is a proud mom of two teenage children. In her free time, she enjoys traveling the world, attending live concerts, going to museums, and hiking. Jennifer lives with her family in Meridian, Idaho.

Social media links

Instagram:

- @Jennifer_Michelle_Coaching (Coaching Program)
- @FamilyCounselingServcies (Counseling Agency)
- @LightBulbEffect (Book)
- @The_Finance_Diet (Book—coming soon!)

LinkedIn:

- @FCSmeridian (Counseling Agency)
- @JenniferMichelleCoaching (Coaching Program)

Facebook:

- www.facebook.com/JenniferMichelleCoaching
- www.facebook.com/TheLightBulbEffect/
- www.facebook.com/TheFinanceDiet
- www.facebook.com/FCSmeridian/

Blogs

- Wellness Blog: https://fcsmeridian.com/wellness-blog
- Business Coaching Blog: https://jennifermichellecoaching.com/?blogcategory=JMC+Business+Blog

Websites:

- www.JenniferMichelleCoaching.com (Coaching Program)
- www.FCSmeridian.com (Counseling Agency)
- www.LightBulbEffect.com (Book)
- www.TheFinanceDiet.com (Book—coming soon!)

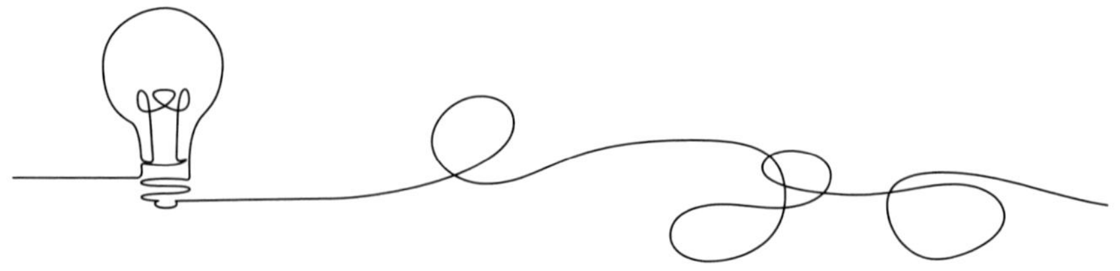

BY JENNIFER MICHELLE

COMING SOON!

www.TheFinanceDiet.com

BOOK JENNIFER MICHELLE TO SPEAK AT YOUR NEXT EVENT!

Jennifer Michelle is available to speak at your next event or to your organization or team. Her dynamic and enlightening presentations have already helped hundreds of people keep their light bulbs burning brightly. If you want your group or team to experience the full brilliance of The Light Bulb Effect, contact Jennifer today.

Jennifer will create a customized keynote speech or seminar tailored to your individual organization's needs.

She is available to speak on a wide variety of topics, including:

- Showing up with dynamic authenticity to become a self-leader through achieving your goals.
- Creating and experiencing transformational change to drive the success you desire for yourself and your team.
- Reaching higher to set and accomplish goals that will lead you and your staff to success.

Jennifer's interactive and inspirational presentations guide you through a self-reflective journey, helping you identify goals, desires, and the roadblocks you may face in your journey as a leader or team member in your organization.

Jennifer offers a variety of speaking formats, including:

- **One-Hour Workshops:** A brief introduction to the basics of supervision, business ownership, ethics and/or The Light Bulb Effect.
- **Keynote Addresses:** An inspirational and humorous seminar individually developed based upon your organization's needs.
- **Half-Day Seminars:** A professional presentation on the topic of choice as it applies to your organization.
- **Full-Day Seminars:** An interactive, professional, and inspirational presentation individually developed around your topic of choice.

For a free consultation with Jennifer to help her learn how to assist your organization, contact her at:

www.JenniferMichelleCoaching.com

www.LightBulbEffect.com

Jennifer@JenniferMichelleCoaching.com